Scottish Branch
British Red Cross Society.

HOSPITAL
LIBRARY SERVICE

This library is organised to make available for you during your stay in hospital, books for your diversion.

You are asked to handle the books carefully, and to endeavour that they are not mislaid or lost.

MUSIC
IN
THE WIND

The story of
LÉON GOOSSENS
and his triumph
over a shattering accident

BARRY WYNNE

Souvenir Press

24.12.68.

First published 1967 by Souvenir Press
Ltd., 95 Mortimer Street, London, W.1,
and simultaneously in Canada by
The Ryerson Press, Toronto, 2, Canada

To the Memory of

JOHN HANSLIP

Test Pilot and Music Lover

*Printed in Great Britain by
The Camelot Press Ltd., London and Southampton*

Contents

Illustrations

Author's Note

In this book the task set me was to record the incident, detail and effect of the accident that befell Léon Goossens.

Whereas I have found it helpful and fascinating to interweave both musical and family background, I have not attempted a full biography. This I must leave to a more knowledgeable pen than my own.

I

Catastrophe!

"I WAS dumbfounded. I could not believe it. . . .

"Nothing is as sudden or ugly as an accident—especially following the dedicated search of beauty he and I pursued together, a few days before when recording the Bach Oboe and Violin Concerto.

"I was appalled by the hideous futility and idiocy of human fate, as I was supremely grateful to have been allowed to live and work and play with so dear a colleague."

The date: June 25, 1962. The man: Léon Goossens. The reaction: Yehudi Menuhin. The accident: a car smash.

* * *

Thus the news stunned the music world. But primarily this was a family crisis, the third in a chain of tragedies delivered upon the Goossens. The first, the break-up of younger daughter Corinne's marriage, which had occasioned the close-knit family to withdraw to the island of Malta for a much needed respite, and the second, the death of Léon's elder brother, Sir Eugène, some ten days later.

Let it be said directly. The Goossens family, going back to Grandfather Eugène Goossens the First, who brought his family over from Belgium in 1873, have carved for themselves a unique niche in the history of British music. All of them have been gifted and each of them has devoted a life-time to honing that skill until Léon, the last of the direct male line, has achieved for his instrument, after nearly 6,000 years, its birth and acceptance as a solo instrument.

*   *   *

Actress Jennie, elder daughter of Léon and his wife, former dancer Leslie Burrowes, saw the family off at London Air-port. The strain of the previous few months was temporarily cast aside as they laughed their farewells and departed, leaving Jennie to hold the fort.

It was while pottering about her flat in the early morning of June 12 that the radio announcer's voice burst in upon her reveries to tell her that Sir Eugène Goossens had died in Hillingdon Hospital upon his return from Switzerland, having collapsed on the aircraft.

She felt her heart involuntarily leap within her at the mention of her Uncle Zen and subsided in shock upon the couch in her sitting-room. Her next reaction, a few seconds later, motivated by the feeling of isolation from the family, was to grasp the telephone and dial the number of her fiancé, Brian. When she heard his voice, she blurted out, "Uncle Zen is dead. Isn't it terrible? I must ring Mum!"

Brian, true to the tradition of all good fiancés, lost no time in rushing round and half an hour later they cabled St. Paul's Bay, Malta. All the Goossens loved Zen. He was that kind of man. The fact that the closing days of his career had been marred by a scandal in Australia in no way lessened the affection and esteem in which all members of the family and his friends regarded him.

Not only did he continue the Goossens tradition of con-ductorship, but he also gained immediate recognition as a composer.

The following morning *The Times* saw to it that justice should be done to his not inconsiderable musical career.

"Sir Eugène Goossens, the conductor, and composer, died yesterday in Hillingdon Hospital; he had been taken ill in Switzerland where he had been visiting two of his five daughters. He was sixty-nine.

"Three generations with the name of Eugène have been violinists and conductors, and the family has contributed many musicians of the highest eminence to the profession of whom Léon, the oboist, and Marie and Sidonie, harpists, are still living.

"Eugène Goossens had a considerable tale of compositions to his credit, some of which in his younger days made an impression during the period of flux and experiment that followed the 1914–1918 war, but, as other conductor-composers have found, the business of conducting other men's music induced an eclecticism which the Twentieth Century, for reasons sufficient or insufficient, has been unwilling to accept. Among his most important are the two operas, *Judith* and *Don Juan Manara*, two libretti by Arnold Bennett, both of which had their first performances at Covent Garden in respectively 1929 and 1937. Some early string quartets, including 'By the Tarn' and 'Jack o' Lantern' held their place for some time, but the work most frequently performed in recent years has been the Oboe Concerto (1927) written for and played by his brother, Léon."

* * *

Upon hearing the sad news, confirmed upon Malta Radio, and distressed no less because he knew that Zen had been in failing health for some time, younger brother Léon caught the next plane to London, leaving his family to complete their vacation. Jennie met her father at Heathrow Airport and drove him back, sad and dispirited, to their house in St. Peter's Square, moving in herself in order to supervise the domestic arrangements.

Following the funeral Léon decided it was pointless to

return to Malta and set about busying himself in a bout of feverish musical activity. This took him on Sunday, June 24, to Stevenage in Hertfordshire, where he spent an enjoyable day in the company of the musician, pianist and composer, Elizabeth Poston and her mother.

Following dinner, Léon decided to delay his departure until 11.15 p.m., in order to avoid the heavy, home-going traffic. In fact, as he drove his maroon Borgward Isabella on to the A1, it was to find that the traffic was still in full spate. Under a canopy of bright early summer stars, with the car radio softly playing late night music, Léon drove steadily towards London. Upon the close-down of programmes at midnight he flicked off the radio and in company with other motorists, surged upon the Hendon Way. His thoughts kept turning to Eugène as he cast his mind back to the time when they were boys. Somehow he could not bring himself to believe that his much adored elder brother, who had been a mighty bulwark and pal through their early years, was now, alas, gone for ever.

At 12.40 a.m., Léon Goossens crossed the Edgware Road, turned left into Dartmouth Road—a short cut he knew well from the visits he was in the habit of making to the Elstree Film Studios—then turned right into Sidmouth Road and drew to a halt at the traffic lights. The lights changed, he let in the clutch, slid smoothly through the first and second gears, and was just about to engage in top, when round the bend of the road he saw the headlights approaching. Positioned safely on the near side, his mental processes briefly acknowledged without concern the oncoming vehicle until, suddenly, the first signals of alarm sped to his brain. In the very instant he became aware that the approaching car seemed to be swaying and paradoxically in a moment when time seemed to stand still, yet events became accelerated in the extreme, he realised that the car was going to hit him head on. At that self-same moment his reflexes responded, causing his hands to grip the steering wheel, his body to go rigid, his eyes to shut, and his right foot to clamp down upon the brake pedal. Then came the rending crash of the violent impact.

Even as the headlights disappeared into the bonnet of Léon's car, so unconsciousness briefly turned off the kaleidoscope of images in his brain.

The street, deserted of pedestrians, suddenly filled with alarmed householders from every side, including the person of the local doctor. Léon, drooped across the smashed steering column, hesitantly began the long climb up from the deep pit of oblivion, and gradually became aware of two basic facts. The first that his mouth was full of blood and many loose teeth, and the second that someone was addressing him from the car window. The voice seemed anxious but reassuring, as if floating down from a thousand miles away.

"Don't try to move," the doctor counselled him, "the ambulance is coming," for already Léon was instinctively seeking out the door handle in an attempt to extricate himself from the car which had concertina'd in around him.

Even as he moved his arm, he became aware of the excruciating stabs of pain from the left-hand side of his body, above his heart. It felt as if his chest had caved in. With alarming clarity his numbed senses reminded him of the bullet he had received just under the heart in the first world war, and the pneumonia he had caught in 1949. This was the third time . . . he must be dying! "Oh God, what an awful way to end," and then two further conflicting thoughts beset his brain. Thank Heavens no one else is involved in this, but where, oh where, is Leslie? He felt unutterably alone. It seemed the most frightening moment of his life; he was about to die without a member of the family to help him.

Another rougher voice seemed to penetrate the car and his consciousness.

"What did he have to come out of a drive like that for. . . ."

Although he could say nothing, Léon's instinctive protest welled up within him. If only he could speak. He hadn't come out of any drive!

Then suddenly he heard the really comforting words that bring reassurance to crash victims a hundred times a day. It was the ambulance man; "Come on, old chap. We'll soon have you out of there. Don't worry. You'll be O.K."

A foot was placed on the buckled side of the car and strong hands tore at the crumpled door. Again floating off into unconsciousness, Léon was vaguely aware of being gently eased out of the driving seat, albeit in horrible agony, and his body being coaxed on to a stretcher lying in the road.

It seemed only a second before the big doors of the ambulance clamped together, the bell jangled its insistent alarm, and the vehicle smoothly raced forward. Léon clearly retained an impression that a sense of urgency was gripping the driver. Obviously they could not tell what damage was concealed beneath his summer-weight jacket, and after all he was a man of sixty-five.

His next recollection was of lights and people looking down at him. He was fighting the sister, who was gently inserting a tube in his nose.

"Come on, now," she said reassuringly. "You must let me do it, I'm trying to help you."

A telephone rang in the small room of the duty house surgeon. He was a compact young man, even diminutive, in his early thirties and full of charm. The voice on the other end of the line said:

"Sorry to disturb you again, a serious accident, name of Léon Goossens . . . a famous Hollywood producer."

As Léon remarked afterwards, the incorrect "Hollywood producer" tag had obviously indicated to the lower echelons of Willesden General Hospital that he might be worth saving!

It was about 2 a.m., that Jennie, in bed in her flat, became aware in the deepest trough of her sleep, of the insistent ringing of the telephone bell. As she moved from under the eiderdown her first instinctive mood of irritation was rapidly swept aside by an obtrusive feeling of alarm, as she glanced at her watch and realised that her disturbance was occasioned by someone calling her in the dead of night. When the voice identified itself as a sergeant from Hammersmith Police Station, Jennie was jolted to full awareness.

"Is that Miss Goossens?" he enquired. "We were given your telephone number by the people in the flat on the ground floor."

When he received an affirmative reply, he continued.

"I am afraid your father has been involved in a serious car accident and Willesden police have asked us to contact you. They suggest you should go straight to Willesden General Hospital."

Jennie, in an onrush of shock, could not prevent an exclamation of "Oh my God! How bad is it?"

At this the sergeant remained detached and unemotional. "He has not regained consciousness yet. The best thing you can do, Miss, is to get down to the hospital."

With a sense of panic creeping over her, she almost threw down the telephone receiver, only to lift it again in the instant. Brian! That very morning, Jennie had moved out of her father's house and back into her own flat, so that fortunately Brian was not too far away. Nervously her fingers manipulated the dial until half-way through she mis-selected a digit and had to start all over again. Her fiancé, alas, seemed lost in the depths of slumber. Just as she was about to give up and personally rush round to his quarters, his sleepy voice muttered an almost incoherent "Hello".

"It's Jennie. Dad's had an accident. I've got to get to Willesden Hospital . . ."

Even before she had finished her sentence, full realisation of these brief words brought Brian to immediate attention.

"O.K., darling. Don't worry. I'll be round in a moment or two."

As Jennie replaced the receiver, she felt a wave of relief and grasping a brush tore at her hair, at the same time searching out her clothes. In not much more than eight minutes and while she was wriggling her toes into her shoes, the doorbell rang, and with hardly a word between them, the two young people dashed out into the cold and cheerless street.

       *   *   *

At the hospital, in the casualty department, Léon Goossens' eyes flickered open. He felt remote from his surroundings and was only distantly aware of the activity about him. Glaring arc lamps seemed to be stabbing into his brain, masked faces stared down at him at very close proximity. He was aware, rather than felt, the injections that went into his arm.

"Right, Sister. I think we're ready now," the surgeon said, followed almost immediately by another voice that he somehow knew belonged to a policeman.

"Blimey, doctor, do you know who this is? He's a C.B.E.!" and then the shutters came down.

The police had also managed to contact Léon's eldest sister, Marie Goossens, the harpist, and she arrived some minutes before the operation was due to begin.

Even as children, Marie had always been the little mother, fussing over her young charges, keeping them spick and span, and generally out of trouble.

The surgeon, already gowned, came out to say a word.

"Don't worry. He's been knocked about a good bit but I think he'll be all right. He's certainly suffered some broken ribs and a pretty bad gash in the mouth. He's lost most of his teeth, I'm afraid."

Marie flinched.

"You know he's an oboe player . . . probably the best in the world. Please do everything you can for his mouth . . . and try to save his teeth."

There was a pause for a second or two.

"Of course," he rejoined, and with that turned on his heel to begin his long night's task.

*   *   *

Jennie was driving her mother's car and she and Brian were hopelessly lost in the deserted streets of north-west London. Brian, an actor with the Old Vic, had only arrived back from Holland that morning. Both of them were seized with frustration and anxiety, not knowing whether Léon was alive or dead, but frantic to reach his bedside. Twenty minutes later they found the hospital, hurled themselves out of the car and ran inside. The anticlimax was complete. They were ushered into a grey waiting room to find Marie and her son, Anthony, calmly whiling away the anxious moments.

"Hello, dear," Marie greeted her niece comfortingly. "I'm sure he'll be all right, but it's . . . it's his mouth."

"How bad is he . . . ?"

"Quite serious. He's broken some ribs, but it's his mouth I'm so worried about. . .!"

In half an hour they had run out of cigarettes.

In the operating theatre the staff worked methodically through the long hours, gradually bringing order out of seeming chaos. The young surgeon sutured the wounds, taking infinite care, finally inserting 150 stitches into the lacerated mouth. He also diagnosed three broken ribs and a cracked sternum.

*   *   *

Just how important was this oboe player, lying inert on the operating table of Willesden Hospital, as the jet black predawn darkness reluctantly gave way to the first probing

B

fingers of dawn. Way back on June 12, in 1928, America's *Musical Courier* greeted the young Léon Goossens with the following caption:

"Hailed as the world's greatest oboist, who is coming to America this month, promises to raise tremendous interest in this, the most beautiful of all reed instruments."

Reporting his first concert, the *New York American* on January 23, said the following:

"Léon Goossens is a master of the instrument, for he makes the most of its limitations in tone colouring, moodal expression and technical variety. He has wonderful delicacy in attack and his breathing is managed with such imperceptible changes that he almost beguiles the listener into imagining the oboe to be capable of voicing long-sustained melody without breaks. Musicianly taste, perfect rhythm, and flawless fingering are other characteristics of Goossens' distinguished reed."

Even five years before that on February 26, 1923, when Léon was twenty-six, *The Times* critic had said this of a Mozart Concert in Wigmore Hall:

"The best thing by far was Mr. Léon Goossens' playing in the quartet for oboe. The unique colour of the oboe is a delight in the orchestra, but never having been much cultivated as a solo instrument, it has not as a rule, endured to have greatness thrust upon it for more than a few moments. Mr. Goossens has so cultivated it, and we must confess to having waited for his every entry with breathless interest. His whole range of 2½ octaves is perfectly capable and uniform, and he can do musically just what he likes with any and every note of it."

The fact is that this oboe player, when listening to his very earliest recordings made in the late '20s and early '30s, is humorously aghast at some passages that lack his present fluency and tonal colouring, which he now demands of himself after sixty years of playing.

*   *   *

At 6 a.m., with the sun creeping up behind the dark buildings of Willesden, two policemen entered the grey painted waiting room and enquired of Jennie if she would care to go to the scene of the accident, to reassure himself that the skid marks on the road confirmed, beyond any question of doubt, that her father had been driving reasonably and accurately on his side of the road.

Jennie was pleased to agree. When they arrived it was to find that the vehicles had been removed, but the evidence of the incident lay shouting on the road surface, in burnt rubber skid marks for all to see. The policemen, experienced decipherers of such tell-tale patterns, explained just what must have happened. They then diffidently suggested that perhaps it might be as well if she examined her father's car. It had already been deposited at a garage and when she saw the Borgward, a fresh wave of anxiety for her father's life seized upon her, for she could hardly credit that any driver could possibly have been extricated from such a tangled mass of metal without having lost his life. There was no doubt that only the soundness of the construction of the vehicle had prevented a complete concertina. The force of the impact of chest and mouth upon the steering column had actually broken the steering wheel. Jennie decided to look no longer, and in a few moments was speeding back to the hospital.

Her return was to coincide with the safe removal of her father from the operating table to the recovery room, the surgeon having done his long night's work well. As the family foregathered once again in the waiting room, the Sister came in and reported that so far so good. The patient would not regain consciousness for an hour or two, and therefore they might safely leave during this period.

Weary, but borne along with a sense of relief, Jennie and Brian returned to the flat, pondering on the best method of breaking the news to her mother in Malta.

*   *   *

It was 8 a.m., on a beautiful Mediterranean morning in St. Paul's Bay, when Leslie and her daughter, Corinne, were interrupted in the midst of their breakfast preparations by the telephone ringing in the hall. With not a passing care, and imagining that friends on the island were giving them an early morning tinkle, Leslie lifted the hand-piece of the instrument. The operator checked the number and requested a moment's pause while he connected London.

The frown that flickered across Leslie's face drew the attention of her daughter, but even before they could exchange a word, she heard Jennie's voice. It sounded strained.

"Is that you, Mum?" she enquired.

"Yes, darling . . ." A tinge of anxiety began to steal upon Leslie's mind.

"Oh, Mum, Dad's had a car accident . . . he's all right," she added instantly, with that touch of hardness to conceal nervousness that no mother could miss in the voice of her daughter.

"How bad is it?"

Jennie was fighting to keep calm, endeavouring to convey an inkling of the seriousness of the situation, without frightening her mother unduly, but Leslie remained strictly composed.

"How bad is he?" she repeated.

"He'll be all right . . . I'm afraid it's his face."

Leslie suddenly knew instinctively that the situation was not good.

"Should I come back?" she enquired, not so much asking the question in practical terms, for already mentally she had packed and gone, but rather to learn from the reaction of Jenny as to just how badly her husband had been hurt.

"Oh yes, I think you should . . . as soon as you can."

Leslie felt a distinct flutter in her heart.

"All right, darling. I'll be on the first available plane."

Even as she replaced the receiver, Corinne, who had been through a considerable emotional strain during the previous few months, was demanding in near desperation to know what on earth had happened. Leslie, showing little outward emotion, was already on the move.

"It's Daddy. He's had a car accident. He's all right, but I must get back to London."

For a split second Leslie paused in her flight to give Corinne a reassuring smile. "Come on, darling, you get on with the breakfast. I must dress." Corinne was almost beside herself with anxiety.

Even as she did so, Leslie began searching in her mind as to who could help her in this moment of crisis. She suddenly thought of their good friend, Hubert Foster Clark. Moving down to the telephone again, she rang his number, but unfortunately there was no reply.

She called through to the kitchen, "The first thing to do is to get down to Luca."

Half an hour later, they tumbled into their motor car.

Even as they were doing so, who should pass by but Hubert, and with an intense feeling of relief, Leslie rushed across to tell him of the accident. Indeed, even before she began to speak, he realised that something was seriously amiss. Anxious to be of assistance, he turned his car and led them at high speed to the airfield. Through his good offices Leslie was shortly to be passenger on a jet winging its way to Rome where she would pick up a connection that would enable her to reach London by tea-time.

*　　　*　　　*

Meanwhile Jennie returned to the hospital and found that her father was occasionally popping his head above the sea of unconsciousness, mercifully insulated from too much pain by a heavy dose of drugs. As she entered the little room, shortly to become over-burdened with flowers from a score of well-wishers, her father's eyes momentarily flickered open, and bending down to kiss him, she whispered, "Don't worry, Dad, everything is going to be fine. Mum will be here in an hour or two."

Even as she said the words, Jennie noticed the reaction, as if a great weight had been taken off his mind, for a ghost of a smile flickered across his face as he shut his eyes to sleep. No longer did Léon Goossens feel that unutterable sense of loneliness which he had experienced on the stretcher. Certainly he would be all right!

At a quarter-to-four in the afternoon, Jennie once again climbed into her mother's car, and slipping through the traffic, made her way to London Airport. She was nervous of her mother's reaction, but when Leslie came tripping through the Customs' shed, her daughter was amazed at her apparent calmness. Indeed, Leslie was exercising all her old professional dancer's skill, remaining outwardly detached and controlled, endeavouring to hide, except in her eyes, the frightful anxiety which seized at her heart.

"Hello, Mum, he seems much better this morning. Come on, we'll drive straight to the hospital."

Leslie looked suntanned and beautiful, slipped her arm through Jennie's and together, mother and daughter sped the last few miles to Léon's bedside.

2

Early Days

LÉON GOOSSENS had been born in Liverpool sixty-five years previously to the very month, and he had been an oboe player for fifty-five of them. However, he could by no means be described as an "old man", indeed, if the casual observer were asked to guess his age, there is little doubt that they might diffidently have suggested that he was about to depart from his forties. A lifetime of disciplined living, hugely enjoyed, a second serene marriage, and many outdoor occupations, he had weathered the years, or rather brushed them aside, with ease and gaiety. Nevertheless, as a boy in May 1902 he had watched the return of the British troops from the South African war, indeed trotted alongside them in the street with a "wide-awake" hat plonked upon his head.

Léon's great-grandfather was born in the architecturally magnificent city of Bruges on May 20, 1793, and his birth is recorded in the register of the church of Notre Dame. As the sun slips across the sky, the shadow of the spire will mark out a house at the corner of the Rue Notre Dame and the Rue du Bourge, a yellow house with shuttered windows and Flemish gables. The family was devoutly Catholic. Léon's great-grandfather began as a jeweller's apprentice and ended as a master silversmith. As if by a marriage of trades, Léon's mother's grandfather was also a master silversmith.

Eugène Goossens the First, as the family would describe him, was born in 1845 and he and his brother showed an early talent for music. As it happened, the choirmaster of Notre Dame, M. Mechelaere lodged in the Goossens household. He shortly discovered that the two boys, aged nine and ten, possessed beautiful voices, so he decided to take them under his care, place them in his choir and foster their musical education.

Mynheer Mechelaere announced that they were "born musicians". At the age of nine, the young Eugène began to take violin lessons at the Bruges Conservatoire and after only two years he won the Medal of the Société Renaissance. He and his brother graduated to the Conservatoire Royale in Brussels, where Eugène studied under Meerts and Beumer.

The renowned Director of the Conservatoire was Fëtis, the celebrated musicologist and teacher of composition, and he was eventually to grant a Certificate of Excellence to young Eugène. At nineteen years of age he won the Premier Prix of the Conservatoire for violin playing, besides distinguishing himself in solfège, harmony, counterpoint and composition. Here was a young virtuoso in the making who would not only excel himself but would pass with his blood a rich vein of musical talent that would descend down the line from generation to generation.

Having graduated from the Conservatoire with distinction, he met and fell in love, as his great-grandson Léon was to do half a century later, with a beautiful young dancer, one Célenie van Dieghem. She was later to become known in London as Madame Sidonie, whose name was also to be passed on to Léon's youngest sister.

While his parents were on tour in 1867, Léon's father, Eugène the Second was born in Bordeaux. By the time he was six years old, the plight of touring musicians on the Continent had become a sad one, and matters came to pass that a decision of great seriousness had to be taken by his parents. There was hardly a living to be obtained by his young violinist father, but rumour had it that conditions in England were that much better. Consequently the family moved lock, stock and barrel, without any security or introductions for the future, to the smoke-begrimed city of London.

It was a cold and cheerless winter in 1873. The fate that has so often befallen the aspiring emigrant descended upon Eugène Goossens the First. He found the greatest difficulty in attracting any attention, and was forced to eke out a bare existence in the gay nightspot of those days at Cremorne Road, Chelsea, but not despairing he later managed to gain entrance to the orchestra of the Covent Garden Opera House.

At one time his ambition was to become a violin concert-soloist, but latterly his interest, helped along by his exacting Continental musical education, became focused and fascinated by the role of the conductor.

He began to observe more closely those under whom he was playing, studying the scores from a new and objective standpoint, familiarising himself with the wide range of currently popular music. His interest, although not entirely appreciated by the Covent Garden management, did not at least escape their attention, and when one day impresario Kate Santley found herself at the last moment without a conductor for one of her London seasons of operetta, she sought the advice of the manager of Covent Garden. He in turn mentioned the young Belgian violinist who had but lately joined the orchestra, and so of a sudden Eugène the First found himself earning the princely sum of £1,000 per annum, conducting *Olivet*, *La Périchole*, *La Marjolaine* and *Orphée aux Enfers*.

Critical acclaim as well as good fortune suddenly descended on the shoulders of the *émigré*, and was all the more heartily endorsed when it was learned that the young conductor had never before carried a baton!

Gradually Eugène Goossens the First established a sound reputation and found himself engaged by the Comedy Opera Company Ltd., as conductor of its Opera Comique in the Strand. The manager was Rupert D'Oyly Carte Senior, founder of the D'Oyly Carte Opera Company, of Gilbert and Sullivan fame. From this entrée it came about that in May 1878, Eugène's efforts for his family were crowned by his conducting a gala performance of *H.M.S. Pinafore* in the presence of Her Majesty, Queen Victoria.

Sidonie, Eugène's wife, was not to be outdone in spite of the fact of her motherhood. In 1882, after several years of touring, she appeared as the leading dancer in Offenbach's *La Belle Hélène*, and *Genevieve de Brabant*. In the late '80s Eugène joined the Carl Rosa Company as second conductor, and his wife devised and produced many of the ballets for the new operas that they staged. She was the toast of the balletomanes of the day, and her fame certainly rivalled that of Adeline Genée, her successor of thirty years later, who has just had a theatre built in her honour at East Grinstead, in Sussex.

The now established conductor's son, Eugène the second, aged sixteen, Léon's father, was despatched to the Brussels Conservatoire, having received his earlier training at the College of St. Louis in Bruges. In Brussels he found himself in the class of Gevaert for composition and Cornélis for the violin. The former had succeeded Fétis as the director of the Conservatoire. Discipline among musical students in those days was complete, if not fearsome. Thus they built their careers on the most exacting foundations, which in later life, so far as the Goossens family was concerned, proved to be their making.

In 1889, Carl Rosa died and Eugène Goossens the First succeeded to the principal conductorship of the company. Grandfather Eugène was an exacting conductor, striving after artistic standards which, alas, were unattainable. The following anecdote is typical of many that surrounded his name.

A Russian bass, whose Mephistopheles was considered his masterpiece, had been engaged just prior to Rosa's death. He did not show up at the rehearsals of *Faust*, and sang his part at the first performance so badly that Eugène called him in for a special rehearsal. The renowned basso objected to being so frequently pulled up that he lost his temper, and said that he had sung the role of Mephistopheles in all the great capitals of the world, under the batons of many great conductors, "whose boots *you*, Mr. Goossens, are not fit to brush!" He added, "I know the part upside down", to which Goossens tartly replied, "That's quite evident. But we don't play it that way in this company!"

Léon's father returned to England after Carl Rosa's death and his father generously invited him to become leader of the second violins. Also, as a test of his progress, Eugène the First invited him to conduct *The Marriage of Figaro*, which task the young twenty-two-year-old conductor, sporting a beard to conceal his tender years, undertook with enthusiasm. However, Grandfather Goossens decided that the young man required further academic study and enrolled him at the Royal Academy of Music in London.

Reluctantly suffering a two-year return to studentship, the young Eugène studied harmony, counterpoint and composition under Davenport, until he eventually returned to the colourful life of the opera company and thereupon immediately fell in love with the young contralto, Annie Cook, of the famous theatrical family, whom he married in 1892.

Léon's mother had been born in Boston, Mass., on June 28, 1860, the year that the American Civil War broke out, while the family were on tour, for her father Aynsley Cook—a descendant of the famous sea "Captain" and navigator—was principal bass with the Carl Rosa Company.

Annie had continued in the footsteps of her father and joined the chorus at Covent Garden, then called the Italian Opera, at the age of fifteen.

The two families were probably contributing a unique effort to Covent Garden, for there were no less than four of them working in the company, Eugène the First was conducting the orchestra, Eugène the Second, Léon's father, was playing principal second violin, Aynsley Cook was singing the bass leading roles and his daughter, Léon's mother, the small contralto parts.

It was in 1893 that Grandfather Eugène, tiring of life with the opera, resigned from the Carl Rosa and settled down to voice teaching in Liverpool. In the meantime, young Annie and Eugène the Second had set up home in Camden Town, in a house adjoining the one in which Crippen was to perform his notorious murder in 1903.

They were blessed by the arrival of twins in 1893 but only the boy child survived and naturally enough he had the mantle of Eugène the Third thrust upon him. The following year Marie Goossens was born, and in 1896 Adolphe. However, the constriction of living in a boarding house with three energetic young children, coupled with the impracticalities of touring such a young family, a decision was made to join Grandfather Goossens, who lived in a roomy old house on Mount Pleasant in Liverpool. It was in this dwelling, overlooking the Brownlow Hill Workhouse—now the site of the new Catholic cathedral—that Léon was born in 1897.

It was not long before the city dwellers decided that with Grandfather Goossens' choir practice rocking the house night after night, and the shrill voices of young would-be singers disturbing the day, that the time had come to seek more open spaces on the far side of the Mersey. They moved to Liscard on the Wirral peninsula, which at that time offered nothing but open fields, firm white sand and the pure sea air of Wallasey and New Brighton.

As a backdrop to this wonderland for children, there rose the distant purple outline of the mysterious Welsh mountains. Not far away were the lonely sand-dunes of the Dee, whose wide estuary gave protection to great flocks of geese in the cold harshness of the winter, and inland stretched the gentle windswept countryside towards Bidston Hill. To the north lay the choppy waters of the Irish Sea and when the young family stood on Perch Rock Lighthouse on a Saturday, they could watch the big steamers, tramps and sailing ships arriving from romantic ports all over the world.

In those days there was no Harbour Board building, nor even that landmark of the north-west, the Liver Building. There were only the big shipping offices of Water Street and the warehouses of Back Goree and the old Custom House, which with St. Nicholas Church and a jumble of quaint buildings, formed the picturesque façade of a fine city.

In 1899, the year in which Léon's father accepted the conductorship of the Carl Rosa Company, the last member of Annie and Eugène the Second's family was born, a sister to Léon. They called her Sidonie. Thus the young family was complete, born into an atmosphere in which the worship of God and music was the sole motivation for life.

3

The Aftermath

WHEN LÉON's eyes next flickered open, it was to see Leslie standing smiling at his bedside. It was a few moments before he could connect the sequence of events and appreciate the fact that his wife, even during the brief interval of his loss of consciousness, had been magically transported from a remote island in the Mediterranean to his hospital bedside in grimy north London.

As he attempted to move in a gesture of greeting, a thousand pains stabbed at his chest and the effort to return her smile felt as if he were about to burst open the patchwork of stitches so meticulously inserted by the surgeon. However, his eyes always dancing reflectors of light, conveyed his relief and pleasure that Leslie had returned to him. Then he saw the flowers. Heaps of them crowding the room, bright with the promise of summer, encouraging him that his friends were wishing him well. But for Leslie, watching her husband overcoming the after-effects of his operation, there could be no doubting the full significance and extent of his injuries.

For an oboe player, however disciplined and tutored over half a century of playing, must nevertheless be served by supple and responsive muscles of both the diaphragm, the larynx and the mouth. In particular the muscles of the lower lip must exert pressure against the reed to obtain a perfect embouchure, and the lips in their turn require the support of the teeth.

The medical report from the Casualty Registrar of the hospital described Léon Goossens' injuries as follows:

"A transverse laceration four inches in length on the chin extending through all layers of the soft tissues into the mouth to involve part of the lower jaw at the site of the attachment of the mucosa to the periosteum of the mandible; many teeth also injured. X-rays reveal thoracic injuries with fractures of the 5th, 6th and 7th ribs on the right with the left rib anteriorly. The fracture of the lower part of the sternum without displacement. Also a linear atelectasis at the left base and sited in the right mid-zone consistent with pulmonary contusion, a small degree of right pneumothorax. The patient has lost all his lower incisor teeth."

To Leslie listening to the professional recital of her husband's injuries, came a deep foreboding that this accident in his sixty-fifth year must inevitably bring to a premature conclusion Léon's brilliant career. Nevertheless, lying awake that night pondering the disaster, she came to realise that if such was the fact, for Léon his life would be over. She therefore determined within herself that whatever else happened, she would remain stubbornly optimistic, and however depressed her husband might become, she would contain her own thoughts and emotions, protecting him from all anxieties, encouraging him at all times, and if necessary, gently to bully him. She slipped into a disturbed and shallow sleep, too wrought up to surrender her mind completely, but thanking God that Léon was at least alive and certain to recover.

Never had the serenity of a holiday in Malta been so rudely shattered as by the events that they had lived through in the last few weeks. However, that island was yet to repay them.

* * *

Léon Goossens was to spend two weeks in Willesden General Hospital until he was released, possibly a little prematurely, on July 5 when he returned to his house in St. Peter's Square. The following day his private practitioner came round to see him and realised that although his wounds were healing well, Léon was suffering considerably from nerves and shock following his accident. He complained of considerable pain in the head and jaw, in addition to paraesthesia in the lip. He seemed agitated and depressed, reporting that he was quite unable to sleep at nights. The doctor immediately commenced treatment, realising that the task of recovery would not be an easy one.

Indeed by this time, having recovered from the immediate after-effects of his experience, Léon had had sufficient time to take stock of his situation. He knew better than anyone else just what the numbness in his lip could mean. He was not frightened for himself, for he had spent more than his fair share of time in the trenches in the first world war, but he was terrified for his family. He in his turn determined that neither Leslie nor his daughters should learn of his deep-seated anxiety.

One of his first requests upon reaching home was that the reed should be extracted from his oboe and placed beside him. When he was alone, and certain that he would not be disturbed, he would place that slender and personally fashioned object between his lips to see if he could effect an embouchure. He was not encouraged by this action and descended into the deep pit of despair.

However, not many hours later he received a visitor armed with a little liquid medicine in the shape of a bottle of Scotch. It was the flautist, Gordon Walker, a lifelong friend who managed the Sinfonia of London orchestra, one of whose tasks is to record film music. His message was simple and to the point. "Get well soon, my dear Léon, we cannot afford to be without you. Don't worry, however difficult it may seem, you can come and practise with the boys."

It was a generous offer with deep understanding from an old friend whom Léon had first met in 1913 when they played together under Nikisch. It was a positive gesture, for neither Gordon Walker nor Léon Goossens were under any misapprehensions, for the oboe is the most difficult of all wind instruments to play, even under ideal circumstances.

Left alone again Léon fretted in an agony of frustration. Always an active man, as much at home on the tractor, with his horses or behind a gun, he had spent a lifetime as the devoted breadwinner of the family, and the thought that he might now be unable to meet such a role filled him with dread. To add to his worries the failure of Corinne's marriage and her little boy, Dominic was an added responsibility and burden—albeit in many respects a happy one.

It was a few weeks later that Leslie and her daughters came to a decision. Léon was not progressing. Now it was the time to take up the very kind offer of Hubert Clark for Léon to convalesce in his lovely villa in Malta.

Once more they trooped to the airport, Jennie, Corinne with little Dominic seeing them safely on their way. Packed carefully into his case was Léon's oboe, to which he had dedicated his life and to which instrument he was determined to return.

c

4

The Oboe

THE OBOE has oft been described as the queen of orchestral instruments. Certainly she is thought of affectionately as being in the feminine gender. Arthur Clappe, the writer of *Acknowledged treatise of the Wind-band* describes the oboe as being "The Feminine sex amongst wind-instruments—quite coquettish, variable as woman-kind in general." She is certainly the most difficult of the woodwinds to play. Her notes are of the purest and it is not without reason that the orchestra, preparatory to tuning their instruments, call upon the oboe player for an A. All other instruments at once accept her ruling and adjust themselves to her royal requirement.

The oboe in various primitive forms has been known for thousands of years and has been found in many distant corners of the earth.

It is of Hindu origin, although traces of her may be found in the sculpture and paintings of ancient Egypt and Greece.

"He tore out a reed, the great God Pan,
From the deep cold bed of the river . . ."

Pipes and reed-pipes, the early ancestors of the modern flute, clarinet and oboe, were fashioned and played upon by primitive people. A complete set of reed-pipes (including a treble, a tenor and a bass) were found in an ancient Egyptian tomb of the 4th dynasty—that is about 3,700 years before the birth of Christ. According to Groves, "although some of these instruments were undoubtedly rude, yet others—both in design and workmanship—were of high class, and it is therefore impossible to speak of the modern oboe as an invention of any particular date."

Undoubtedly the oboe is the most ancient of the reed instruments; it has come down to us without undergoing any radical changes of form; ancient specimens are all conical, varying only in their proportions as to length and width at the bell.* Its more modern image may be traced back to the Brahmin epoch from the twelfth to the seventh century B.C., when it was called the *otou*. Although still played in India today, this is a most primitive oboe.

The Burmese and Mongols also have an oboe which is attributed to great antiquity. It is somewhat similar to the *otou*, but in reality is a long, straight trumpet with a flaring bell which is played with a very strong double reed. Some of these instruments may extend to eight or nine feet, and the sound emitted from them by the Mongols carries over a tremendous distance.

A similar oboe is found in Japan and China, and closely resembles its Indian relation. In a record of instruments used in China written by the Emperor Kang-hi he mentions the oboe which they called a *koan*. It had a single reed rather than a double and its sonority imitated a small child's cry.

The Malays have a large oboe called a *straoni*, while the Siamese called theirs a *Pi-Chanai*, while on the other side of the world, a primitive oboe called a *chirimia* was known in Mexico. It was much used on the plateau of Tenochctitlan.

However, historians seem generally to agree that the Pelasgians, related to the Hindus, brought to Hellas the cultivation of the reeds. No doubt the Greeks received their instruments from the Lydians and Phrygians, whose

* L. Pillaut.

ancestors had emigrated from Persia. Greek texts are quite explicit concerning reed instruments. They knew both the single and double reeds as used in the oboe and called it the *zeugos* (the joining of two equals, i.e. two reeds). Aristotle in 380 B.C. described the technique of the *auloi* (*tibia* in Latin), the name for the reed instrument:

"The reeds of the *auloi* must be compact, smooth and uniform, in order that the column of air which passes through them may also be smooth, uniform, and uninterrupted. That is why the *zeuge* moistened with saliva has a more mellow tone, while when dried it has a coarse tone, for the air which traverses the moist, smooth body is soft and uniform. The proof is that the breath itself, when it is moist, will strike less hard against the *zeuge*, and be dispersed, but if dry it will adhere to the reed and make the attack rougher."

The reed of the oboe is what the larynx is to the human voice. The modern reed is harvested from the marshlands bordering the Mediterranean, but the Greeks selected theirs from Lake Orchomenus: "They say, and it seems to be true, that when the water in the Lake Orchomenus is higher the cane attains its full length the first year, but that it does not arrive at maturity until the following year, if the water remains at the same level.

"The cane which has reached maturity is the one that is used to make the *zeuge*, while the cane from which the water has receded is the *Bombycious* (the cane for pipes). They say that the *zeugite* cane differs in particular in that it has more body, is fuller, fleshier, and has, on the whole, a feminine appearance."

Before the time of Antigenide—380 B.C.—when Greek music was without ornament, the cane for the reeds was cut in the month of Boedromion, at about that rising of the constellation Bootes (mid-September). The cut cane could not be used until several years later; it became suitable only after a long preparation, and the opening of the reeds contracted, which was necessary for ordinary playing. "But when they began to have 'figured music', the time of the cutting was changed, for now they cut the cane in the month of Scirrophorion or Hecatombeon (June), a little before the summer solstice, or even at that season. It could be used at the end of three years. . . ."*

The oboe first appears in English history about the time of the reign of Henry III, 1216–72, and then it was known as a shawm or wayt, and was used for signalling purposes by armed night-watchmen. At this period, however, it was by no means a refined and sophisticated instrument. It was also found in Wales, being a large oboe called a Pibgorn which was played by wandering musicians. It is known that the peasants on the island of Anglesey danced to a tune on this instrument which was dubbed the Pibgorn.

It would seem that the introduction of the oboe to Europe came about in the following manner. As history records, the Aryan race became divided into Indian and Persian and there is little doubt that the instrument originated in the former country and was either received or carried away by their relations, the Persians. In due course of time, this nation was overcome by the Arabs and we know that in the Arabian orchestra the oboe featured predominantly, and was called a *zourna*, *sourna*, or *sournay*, but today is generally called a *zamar*. Its performance is described thus in Freytag's Arabian dictionary, "cecinit organo, quod ore inflatur", which translated gives a very accurate description of oboe playing, "one sings with the instrument into which one plays with the mouth". It was the returning Crusaders who brought back to Europe these musical instruments as well as the sentimental and martial music of the Saracens.

Without doubt it was in France that the oboe found its west European home, and throughout the last four or five centuries it is Frenchmen who have brought to the instrument distinction, not only of its building but also of its

* Gevaert, ibid.

playing. Lulli wrote oboe marches for the musketeers of King Louis XIV, the French Guards and other regiments, which may be found in the library of Versailles. At this time the military musicians were called "Hautbôistes" among players of the high wood.

In 1671 Cambert introduced the oboes into the orchestra of the Paris Opera. They were in equal number to the violins, namely twelve, and from that time onward they became part of the orchestra in this theatre.

At the museum of the Paris Conservatory one may see oboes of the seventeenth century which are masterpieces of workmanship and the Handel Sonatas (1738) confirmed that by this time the technique of the oboe was already advanced.

It was towards the middle of the eighteenth century that the oboe de cassia (hunting oboe) later called cor anglais (English horn in England) began to appear in orchestral music. It was made of wood covered with leather. Its curved or pear-shaped bell was the same as our modern cor anglais and now the great composers began to make use of the instrument. In 1767 Gluck used it in his Italian *Alceste*, while Bach used the English horn in his cantatas and in his *Christmas Oratorio*. Wagner was the first, in his opera *Lohengrin*, to use the English horn throughout a work.

After the death of Handel, it seems that the horn fell into comparative disuse until revived by such modern composers as Richard Strauss in his *Symphonia Domestica*, and by Debussy and Ravel.

It was in about 1750 that the first oboe virtuosos began to attract notice, the Besozzi brothers in Italy, and Sallentin in France, the latter being named Professor of the oboe in 1795. He was later to be succeeded by Vogt, Verroust, Triebert, Colin and then Gillet, who brought the technique of the oboe and reed-making to the highest degree of perfection, and whose descendant until recently played in one of the famous American orchestras.

So far as the manufacture of the instrument is concerned, substantial improvements in the design and the construction of the oboe were made at the end of the nineteenth century by Delusse. When he died his tools and models came into the possession of Brod, who wrote of the Delusse oboe ". . . they excelled in the accuracy, homogeneity, and beauty of tone". However, Brod and his brother decided to take the manufacture of this instrument still further ". . . hoping to improve it still more, to make the study of it easy, and to make it known, as the first of the wind instruments deserves to be known".

In fact, the present form of the English horn is a direct descendant of Brod's oboe ". . . the tone of which was warm and generous, resembling the human voice". Whereas Brod had a preference for the use of boxwood, it is more usual nowadays to construct them of ebony. The modern oboe, a direct and little changed descendant of the original, is an instrument that has been brought to the highest degree of perfection, thanks to the loving care and skill of instrument makers over the centuries.

It now has a range of three octaves and its compass includes over 100 fingerings. The modern oboe has an exact length of 580 mm. including the bell. Within this body or "bore" are a series of frustrums or chambers of resonance ending in the bell, which is flaring and slightly hyperbolic, and has an opening of exactly 36 mm. wide, but it is the reed which sets the air in vibration, and measures some 25 to 27 mm. in length. It is grown abundantly in the Mediterranean and particularly in Provence.

The oboist will make his own reeds, lavishing much care and attention upon them. In fact it is still necessary to leave the rods (canes) for three years after cutting. They will then be split into three parts and reduced in width. Next they must be gouged or hollowed to exact, indeed critical, proportions, finally being shaped with such precision that one stroke of the knife, too little or too much can change the entire tone of the instrument. Eventually the reed will be nicked by the knife in an exact position, bent back and thus will become a twin or double reed, which will transport the wind from the lungs of the oboist in meticulous vibration down into the instrument to produce that wondrous sound that sings alone above the orchestra, speaking directly to the soul and bringing, so often, the heart to tears.

The fashioning of the delicate reed, so vital to the instrument, is an exact science. The reed should neither be too soft nor too hard, for the high notes may not come out easily or the low notes will recede. It is possible that the reed could have no timbre or no vibration. Conversely it may be too shrill and too brassy and, finally, the reed itself will have to be tuned. The precision required from the reed is so exact that when the cane is cut it has to include two joints, because it has been found over the centuries that the joints on the same stem are "naturally" in harmony, whereas if half the reed were made from one cane and the other half from another, this would not be so.

Léon Goossens has used the same oboe—and this is unusual—for exactly sixty years. It was made especially for him, as we will see, and when playing it it becomes, as it were, his voice. But to produce his distinctive tone, he has to listen with a meticulously attentive ear, in order to create and control that magical sound of the queen of the woodwind instruments.

As has been said, the oboe is the most difficult of the woodwind instruments to play, and a critic, many years ago, decided that he would like to learn just how difficult.

"I spent half an hour in the company of an oboe player and in spite of his careful instructions and the extremely light (as I thought) pressure of my lips on the reed, I never got so much as a whisper."

It is the "embouchure"—that is the approach or address

of the lips to the reed—that in itself is an essential part of the technique. The flat, fragile reed has to be held lightly between the lips and only far enough into the mouth to allow the tongue to touch the top of it slightly. The reed is placed very naturally on the lower lip, this movement making the lower lip cover the edges of the teeth; the oboist then draws the upper lip down over the edges of the upper teeth until it rests against the reed. This description illustrates the fundamental use the oboist makes of his mouth, lips and surrounding muscles.

For Léon Goossens this essential area of sensitivity had now been utterly shattered. Would he ever be able to play again?

5

Malta

LÉON HAD been somewhat quiet and withdrawn during the air journey and as the pilot gently eased the nose of his aircraft forward at the beginning of their long descent approach, Leslie tucked her arm through her husband's. It was the first week in September and the air was perfectly clear. The surface of the sea was a deep cobalt blue, and reflected the dancing shafts of sunlight so that it became an unending vista of sparkling water, broken only by the purple outline of the island for which they were bound.

It had been a long two months since Léon had last visited Malta and, strangely, he approached the period of convalescence with timidity. For Leslie it was the end of something approaching a nightmare, a goal, a hope, a possibility, for her husband was certainly not a good patient.

Whereas he put on a bold front, it was nevertheless plain for all to see that depression and anxiety were holding back his recovery. Physically the damage seemed to be repairing well, although there was paraesthesia in the lip, and on either side there was a certain thickening by scar tissue. The apparent complete lack of sensation in this part of his mouth, the specialist assured Léon, would gradually right itself in the course of time, but to the oboe player, who constantly placed the reed of his oboe between his lips, it felt like utter disaster.

It was as much to take him out of himself and to clear his
mind that Leslie had decided upon their visit to Malta.
Overcoming the seeming reluctance, or at least a general
apathy on the part of her husband, she had decided that
with his fondness for outdoor living the sun and sea would
offer the best hope.

Léon's spirits began to rise when they reached their
destination. He almost became enthused, rather like a school-
boy finally reaching his holiday destination. Always fond of
boats, the prospect of life at close proximity with the sea, was
a pleasing one. Added to this they were made tremendously
welcome by their friends on the island.

After a day or two, Léon decided that in spite of the fact
that he had lost so many teeth he must try and play his
instrument again. He inserted the reed in the oboe and,
while Leslie was out of the villa, he struggled vainly to produce some ordered notes. He was looking for an answer, but
it certainly wasn't there, and once again despondency and
anxiety gripped him. Throughout his life Léon had always
felt a distinct responsibility to his family.

How on earth was he going to be able to support them,
and young Dominic Spence, his grandson was not yet one
year old with no father to look after him. In a way it was
made all the more unbearable for Léon because his wife
refused absolutely to maintain anything but the most buoyant
optimism for the future! Never once did she allow her personal
fears to impinge on Léon's thinking. They were both playing
the same game, touchingly and with devotion.

Only once can Leslie recall Léon actually voicing his doubt.
It was some days after their arrival when, once again he had
tried to practise on his own. She had re-entered the villa,
just as he was walking out of his bedroom, "It's no good," he
had said to himself despairingly, "I can't do it."

Fortunately, later the same day, matters took a turn for the
better. Léon was visiting the Union Club and was confiding

in a friend the problems that confronted him especially with regard to his teeth. He received an interesting reaction.

"Perhaps I can help you, Léon. I am very friendly with the senior Royal Naval dental surgeon on the island and I am sure he would be happy to advise you."

That gentleman did far more than offer his advice. Not only did he grasp the full implication of the injuries sustained, but he offered to do something towards remedying the defect. He virtually instructed Léon to attend his surgery at Bigi Hospital the following morning and for the next three weeks. Together with his first-class dental mechanic, he set about the emergency orthodontic repair of Léon's mouth. However, it was to take another year of fine specialised treatment on the part of Léon's personal dental surgeon, before his teeth would be fully restored.

Leslie was highly delighted for she believed that this could prove to be a crucial step on his road to recovery and regaining his confidence.

It was while lying in the sun that Léon had time to ponder his predicament and muse upon his life so far. His family were long lived and he was an active and generally robust man. He could not contemplate the thought of giving up work. He was utterly determined that he would be self-supporting. If necessary, he would have to extend his teaching role; he might even have to seek a staff appointment somewhere, although the thought was abhorrent. It was not only the predicament of his family which disturbed him, but also the great sense of loss that he was suffering with the passing of Zen. He had always been very much the younger brother. To a certain extent he had been protected and guided by Eugène, generally studious, self-composed and full of confidence.

And then there had been poor Adolphe, lost to the family in the first world war. How they had missed him, and now, of the men, only Léon remained. Even the name Goossens would soon disappear for, strangely, both he and Eugène had fathered only girl children. It had been such a strong male line, offering so much talent to the world of music, that it was almost inconceivable that now it would take its final bow through him.

Léon's spirit and stubbornness began to assert itself. He would not give in. He still had something to offer. As he lay back in his deck-chair with half-closed eyes, he was transported to a scene very remote from his present place in the Mediterranean sun. He could see as if it were yesterday his youngest sister, Sidonie, being bathed by his mother in the galvanised bath on the flagstones of their kitchen in Liscard near Liverpool. They had been idyllic childhood days. He began to dream.

6

Childhood

It was in 1899 that Eugène Goossens the Second was offered and accepted the principal conductorship of the Carl Rosa Company, while Grandfather Goossens two years previously had taken upon himself the duties of organist and choirmaster of St. Anne's Jesuit Church in the Liverpool suburb of Edge Hill. When Eugène the Third reached the tender age of eight, at about the same time as Léon and Sidonie were being washed in the galvanised bath, it was decided that the little fellow should be sent as a boarder to St. Francis Xavier's School in Bruges.

Eugène was not a strong boy and although he had been sold the adventure in glittering terms, he felt not a little lonely sitting in the corner of a London, Chatham & Dover Railway compartment, together with about one hundred other schoolboys whose parents were intent upon their receiving a Continental education. There is little doubt that the highly sensitive child was called upon to suffer much in the three years that he spent in Belgium. He was frequently ragged, especially by the Flemish boys, for between them and the English there existed an hostility which was difficult to explain.

It was in something approaching horror that Eugène, upon his eventual return home, confided in Léon a description of the occasion when the Flemings cocooned him in a blanket and refused to release him. From that moment on, until his death, he hated having anything placed over his head. He gained the advantage of speaking fluent French and a rather execrable Flemish and, in his third year, he enrolled as a student in the local "Muziek-Conservatorium" where he took violin, piano and harmony lessons, also large doses of solfège.

The years slipped by until it was finally decided by Léon's father that Liscard, pleasant as it was in the country with the fresh sea breezes, was altogether too inconvenient. Consequently, the family moved to another house in Chatham Street, Liverpool, near Abercrombie Square, only a short walk from the Philharmonic Hall. The area was somewhat dingy and the house Victorian, but the children loved it.

To all intents and purposes it was now a family of four, because for eight months in the year papa was on tour with the Carl Rosa, and young Eugène the Third was in Belgium.

The sitting-room of the house, or as it was known, the music room, was warm, typically Victorian and comforting. There was an upright Bechstein, with moth-eaten bullrushes standing in a Chinese jar, and a nasty aspidistra—"The Aspidistra" as Léon is wont to describe it.

There were two bedrooms for the children, dividing the boys from the girls, and the vision of the nursery with their flannelette pyjamas spread out on the guard before a roaring fire, evoked warmer memories for the oboist than ever the Mediterranean sun could produce.

When Léon attained five years of age, a certain Miss Perris began visiting the house in order to give him the first rudiments of the piano, although his father when at home had previously effected an introduction to that instrument. This lady, cold, sallow and dressed overall in black, taught by the rule of a pencil cracking on soft, rebellious knuckles. She wore pince-nez and, by way of reprisal, the children would pull at the cord catching her unawares and almost tearing her nose. They remained her pupils for a long two years.

In due course, Adolphe and Léon were enrolled in the Catholic Institute, a school run by the Christian Brothers, a conglomeration of Irish priests and lay teachers.

Life was highly regimented for the young family. While father was away on tour with the Carl Rosa, their mother not only had to care for the house single-handed, but also to supervise and discipline the young musicians. Before leaving, their papa would draw up a chart for each child so that the hours spent outside school were carefully apportioned into periods of selective study throughout each day.

When Léon's parents were married, Grandfather Goossens had tendered this advice to his son:

"Eugène, if you have children, encourage them to select an unusual instrument. Everyone plays the violin and piano and therefore competition is acute. Teach them these instruments, by all means, but let them specialise in something different. Besides which, it will make all the more fun when they play together in the evenings."

This advice was to be heeded, and it was not long before Adolphe was introduced to the French horn, while Marie began playing the harp.

However it was not until Léon was nearly eight years old that the first mention of the oboe was made, and this in the most subtle of terms. It came about in this manner. Once a year, the Carl Rosa would visit Liverpool on tour and Léon's father would be able to take up residence at home while conducting the repertoire of opera in the Shakespeare Theatre. This would offer several occasions for a family outing.

Opposite the house in cobbled Chatham Street, stood a wonderful livery stable which traded under the name of White. There were coaches, carriages and cabs of all descriptions and the children spent hours peering through the windows observing the morning and evening routine. The boxes were on the top floor and the horses so well trained that at the end of their working day they would be unharnessed, patted on the quarters, at which signal they would troop up the ramp and disappear inside for their evening meal.

The only time the boys were allowed to cross the street was on those occasions when they were to order a cab to take the family, usually upon a Friday or Saturday night, to the theatre to listen to Father conducting the opera. This was a day of intense excitement in the Goossens household.

Léon, full of mischief and brimming-over with energy, was selected first, scrubbed until his cheeks shone, decked up in his Sunday best, be-gaitered, gloved and, with his bonnet firmly tucked down on his head, he would be sat atop the tall chest in his bedroom, from which point it was quite impossible for him to escape to mischief! Then his mother, with the help of Marie, would turn her attention to Adolphe, the rest of the family and finally herself.

Then came the moment of utmost excitement for which they had all been waiting; the arrival from White's of their cab. The horse would exhale warm air into the frosty night, the candle lamps would glow on either side and the moustachioed cabby would look magnificent in his heavy over-coat, carrying his long whip. Mother, protective as ever, would counsel him to hold the horse's head and, with a "mind the horse, dears" the family would scramble in.

With warm rugs tucked round their knees, the sweet smell of the upholstery carrying an unmistakable tincture of manure to their nostrils, Léon, his brother and sister would wait expectantly for the cab to move off. Suddenly the big wheels outside the door would begin to turn, reflected in the candlelight from the lamps, glowing red from the rear. Immediately the rhythm of the iron-clad wheels drumming across the cobbles filled the inside of the cab as they swayed

D

and clattered towards their destination, with the horse's hooves clip-clopping before them.

It was utterly enthralling and when they arrived, far too quickly, at the entrance to the theatre, it was to be met by the resplendent figure of the manager who, showing them the greatest respect, would lead the young family to their box. Off came their topcoats and gaiters, to be carefully stacked at the back, while the children would crowd forward to savour the atmosphere of the people coming in and the orchestra preparing for battle.

The theatre was filled with soft glowing light and an atmosphere of expectation gripped the audience. Then suddenly, with a discreet tap upon the door, the second conductor, Van Noorden, would come into their box and carefully take a seat behind Léon, who sensed no significance in his appearance.

"Good evening, Master Léon, are you looking forward to the opera? This evening we will hear quite a lot from the oboe."

His father had often told him of the oboe and as the magic of Lohengrin began to unfold, he would suddenly feel a hand gripping his elbow.

" Listen . . . here it comes. There . . . can you hear the oboe?"

Little did Léon realise the subterfuge, the magnificent subterfuge, being entered upon by his stern but kindly young father. No pressure here, just the gentlest of persuasion, a subtle introduction that was to be fostered for two whole years before a concrete suggestion would be made that maybe Léon might like to study this instrument.

The opera was a trifle heavy for the young family to maintain their interest throughout, but they were swept along by the music until, their emotions exhausted, there would come a life-saving interval. Then father would magically appear, always carrying a box of chocolates. So the long evening would continue until, dead tired, the young aspiring musicians would struggle down the steps out into the cold night air, and rattle home behind a horse who was equally looking forward to a warm bed and a titbit to eat before dreaming.

When winter gave way to summer, father would stay at home for eight weeks or more, and life would be full of fun. Bearded, like Grandfather Goossens, Eugène the Second unwittingly instilled some fear into his youngest son. He was, nevertheless, gentle and kindly, often talking to him of music as a master might discuss it with his pupil, calling the boy baby of the family affectionately "Lee" and helping him with his problems on the piano.

Then he would sit down at the Bechstein and, with a new operatic score before him, set about memorising each bar of the music, marking in pencil every nuance and inflection of the vocal line. He absorbed each passage in such detail that singers would say, "Once you have coached a role with —E.G., you don't forget it until you die!"

On one memorable day in June 1904, a somewhat severe and introspective young Eugène the Third returned to the fold. After three years' absence at school in Belgium the family was complete again and Zen joined Adolphe and Léon at the Christian Brothers Institute.

The first-born, adored by his parents, was now old enough to enrol at the Liverpool College of Music for part-time violin and piano lessons under Alfred and Charles Ross.

At the height of the summer, Léon's father would reluctantly drag himself away from his flower garden, which had become his all consuming passion, to take the family for a holiday to Wales. For a short time, the rigorous discipline of the home would be broken, or at least relieved, by a change of environment and a slight relaxation in the round of practice and tuition. When they returned, duly refreshed, not only would Father help with all the household chores but he would take upon himself the task of renovating the house, painting it outside and in with thoroughly professional expertise. It was some two years later, just after Adolphe had started French horn lessons with Persch, the solo horn player of the Hallé Orchestra, that Léon was called in to speak to his father on a subject, the introduction of which had been subtly prepared. Papa was sitting in his favourite armchair.

"Come, Lee," he said, holding wide his arms. Unhesitatingly, and filled with affection for this somewhat stern embodiment of Victorian parenthood, Léon sat himself upon his father's knee, for he was always a tiddler and looked far younger than his long eight years.

"I have been thinking; Adie has started playing the horn and I am wondering which instrument you would like to take up?"

With such expertise as one might expect from a professional actor, Father Goossens carried on as if inspired on the moment, "How would you like to take up the oboe?" to which Léon responded in pent-up excitement, "Oh, Dad, I'd simple LOVE it!" And he meant every word of it!

Thus the decision was taken and a wondrous alliance was born between an instrument and a young musician.

At about this time, Adolphe and Léon joined elder brother Eugène for weekly periods of instruction at the Liverpool College of Music, the latter studying the piano under Charles Ross.

He was a middle-aged man who waddled when he walked, had a large head and was clean shaven. Teaching was something of a chore which he reluctantly performed, keeping a watchful eye upon the clock. Nevertheless, he managed to instil the rudiments of piano playing in young Léon until, upon one glorious day, his father arranged that he should start taking lessons from Charles Reynolds, first oboist of the Hallé Orchestra, and the only great English oboe player of his generation.

However Reynolds was the possessor of a weak stomach and a quicksilver temper. In order to help appease the former, he constantly munched charcoal biscuits and when poor Léon fell from grace with a bad note or poor phrasing, his teacher would explode, showering the young would-be oboist in a cloud of charcoal soot.

With Léon's father away once more, life continued its disciplined run. Each Friday a letter would arrive for Annie Goossens containing half a £5 note, to be followed by a letter in a later post with the corresponding half sent separately. Having reunited the gleaming white promissory note of the realm, one of the boys would accompany his mother post-haste to Parr's Bank, which the children misinterpreted as being Pa's Bank and thus assumed that their father was a wealthy man indeed!

The College of Music boasted a sturdy student orchestra, presided over by old Carl Courvoisier, leader of the Liverpool String Quartet. The three young musicians were soon inducted into the orchestra and it was not long before they were fighting their way through the symphonies of Beethoven, Mozart and Schubert. Each week they took a new symphony and thus covered tremendous ground.

Léon became so immersed in the works that even thirty or forty years later, coming to them afresh when playing in an orchestra, he found that he remembered them well. Whereas a colleague might turn to him and say, "I haven't come across this before", Léon could smile, recall his early student days and tender some advice.

But, of all his childhood memories, there was none sweeter than the recollection of Christmas time. Father would return and magic would descend upon the household. With fires burning in the grates in every room, mysterious packets would begin to appear, and Dad could be seen labouring at his task of producing a nativity crib from plain brown paper, much glue and paint. When completed, it was placed in a corner of the room with candles that made it glow. It was perfect in every detail and, as Christmas music filled the Goossens household, gifts were showered upon each child equally. Then, the present giving over, the two eldest boys would venture out into the bleak and frosty streets of Liverpool to sing in Grandfather's famous choir. The church was invariably cold.

Leon shivered. He must have dozed. The sun was already sinking towards the distant horizon and a cool evening breeze awoke him from his reverie. Leslie was no longer in her chair. She suddenly appeared, carrying a tea tray.

"Ah, you're awake, darling."

Léon yawned. "I must have been dozing."

7

First Concert

THE COLOUR of the sea was gradually darkening, and the shadows from the setting September sun were growing longer so that Leslie and Léon decided to go indoors. Upon entering Léon picked up his oboe and dropped into a large, comfortable wicker chair.

"You know, darling, in spite of my sleep, I feel quite tired," he said, laughing.

"What were you dreaming about?" Leslie enquired, as she moved about the cool room which carried the sweet scent of the herbs growing outside.

"Oh, I was thinking of the early days in Liverpool. Do you know, it seems like a different world."

"The world of the aspidistra?"

Léon laughed.

"How I remember that wretched plant. When we were practising, mother used to invariably come in with an excuse that she wanted to wipe its leaves with a damp cloth, but really she was intent on seeing whether or not we were concentrating on our work. Her knowledge of our instruments was fairly limited, and I can remember that if I said to her, 'Mother, I think this is a wrong note just here', she would glance over my shoulder and say, 'Well, er, let me see . . . why, er, yes, dear, *perhaps* it is . . . now I wonder . . . hm! . . .

yes, I am not quite sure . . . (suddenly) well, dear, you will
have to wait until Miss Perris arrives'!"

Leslie burst out laughing.

"Poor Mum, her work was unending; it's strange the
memories one retains. The Liver Building—I remember that.
Before they raised the clock to place it in position they
arranged a civic banquet around it, upturned upon the floor,
so that there were sixty guests, one for each minute on the
dial. There was a photograph in the paper. Then there was
father and his tomatoes. He always used to smoke a pipe and
to cope with the greenfly he would turn it about, place the
bowl in his mouth and blow the fumes out along the stem,
thence all over the plants. It was the nicotine, he said, that
dealt with the greenfly!

"Then I recall the coming of the first little taxicabs
to White's at the livery stable. They were two-cylinder
Renaults, painted bright yellow, and we used to call them
the mustard pots. They marked the end of an era . . . especially for White's and their beautiful horses. The old coach-
man in his greatcoat climbing up on to the stage, taking
out, from beneath a flap on the box on which he sat, his tall
top-hat, the crown of which he would smooth on his sleeve,
with slick dexterity."

There was a pause. Leslie could not quite fathom the
motivation behind Léon's reminiscences but he hadn't
talked so much for some time, and she was happy to listen
to his conversation.

"Was there much laughter in those days?" she enquired.

"Oh, Heavens, yes," he responded, "but not always at
the right things! I well remember Mother taking us to the
zoo at New Brighton Tower. On one occasion we were
looking at the monkeys and, naturally enough, I got a bit
too close. Perhaps I was teasing it, I don't know, but its
hand came through the bars and gave me a jagged cut
across the eye. Poor Mother was beside herself with fury.

All set for action—the Goossens' cricket team, turn of the century. *Left to right*, Adolphe, Sidonie, Marie and Léon behind the wicket.

At home commissioned
and ready for the front,
1918.

The shattered steel
shaving mirror and Ethel
Smyth cigarette case that
deflected the bullet from
Léon's heart.

'The brute,' she cried, 'the brute,' and taking her long-handled black and white parasol, she slipped it through the bars and tried to give the creature a smart crack on the rump by way of retaliation. This the monkey thoroughly enjoyed and, catching her unawares, tore the parasol from her hands, whisking it smartly to the top of the cage forty feet above the ground. The crowd loved it—so did the monkeys! They tore it to shreds, while we children didn't know whether to laugh or cry. Mother could get very angry sometimes.

"There was an occasion, again at the same zoo, when we were observing the lions. One of the great cats suddenly decided to lift its leg against the bar and all four of us were showered at very close range! Fortunately, it missed Mum and on this occasion, thank goodness, she saw the funny side. We all roared with laughter."

Léon fingered his oboe lovingly.

"How well I recall Dad sending away to Lorée in Paris for this. It was shortly after he agreed that I might learn to play the oboe and I think he did it with the object of keeping up my enthusiasm, as much as for the fact that in those days only the French could make the finest instruments. I remember carving my initials on each joint shortly after it arrived so that I would always be able to identify it. They are still there."

Dusk had fallen and Léon had tired himself by talking.

"Have a drink, darling," Leslie counselled him, to which he readily agreed. They decided not to go out that evening but retired early, preparatory to Léon spending another morning in the dental surgery.

Progress was good and some three weeks later, choosing a moment when alone, the oboist tried once more to seek response from his instrument. He was much downhearted after the attempt, for try as he might, the muscles of his lips still failed to respond. They felt stiff, without feeling, in spite of the support they were receiving from the temporary bridge.

Somehow, he had brought himself to believe that matters would now progress well, but he was underestimating the damage he had sustained. He sucked the reed and tried and tried again. It was as if the muscles had disappeared. He prayed that he might yet find an answer.

Léon would agree that he is a religious man although he is not a truly practising Catholic. Nevertheless, his belief in God is rock-firm. More than anything else, Léon Goossens loves to play religious music. Somehow it is an offering direct, outside the field of competition, serene in its inspiration and most often played in a house of God. He needed help now and he was not ashamed to pray for it.

He often found himself thinking of his grandfather in these days, for thoughts of religion always reminded him of choir practice under the stern eye of that maestro of discipline. Eugène the First had died in 1906 when Léon was nine years old. He had made his annual pilgrimage to Lourdes, hoping for a cure of his rheumatism but, on this occasion, he caught a severe chill on the return journey.

On arrival in Liverpool, he had a sudden seizure from which he did not recover. Léon's father and his eldest brother, Eugène, were at the bedside when the old man slipped away. He was a devout Roman Catholic and he had devoted his life in equal proportions to his church and to his music.

It was incredible how the conducting tradition had been handed on from one Eugène to the next. In later years, when carrying the baton for the British National Opera Company, his brother was once handed a score, which had pencilled notations in the hand of both his father and his grandfather. In order to keep the tradition alive, he added a few of his own!

However, Léon's father was no less a stern critic than Eugène the First had been, and it was to be thirty years before the oboist achieved a word of praise from his parent. The days of Léon's infancy would shortly be drawing to a close for, in the following year, he would take part in his first concert and, shortly after this, his eldest brother would win his scholarship to the Royal College of Music in London where, eventually, his brothers and sisters would follow him.

No more those wonderful northern high teas with Mum and Dad in Liverpool. Cold beef, perhaps, to start, or omelette, or fried eggs; mounds of fresh baked home-made bread made by Léon's mother, plenty of butter, jam and syrup which they adored; a large fruit cake, Queen's cakes, rock cakes and pots of steaming tea. The family lived well on £5 a week housekeeping.

The meals would always be happy occasions, with Mum and Dad presiding over the heavily laden table, surrounded by their five young children. Eugène, sitting at his father's right hand, introspective but assured. Never very robust in health, he was nevertheless intellectually the leader among his brothers and sisters. He was something of a lone wolf, reading extensively and already taking his first painful steps in composition. In later life he was to marry three times. Charming, debonair, full of fun, nevertheless he was not to make a successful marriage partner.

Then there was Marie, the little mother, who watched over her flock with an authority which, although sometimes disputed, she somehow managed to maintain by hook or by crook. The younger ones thought of her as being a trifle bossy but, as she grew older, this mantle fell away and now she is adored by both men and women musicians alike. As her brother would say, she is one of the few women in the profession who is invariably kissed when she enters upon the concert platform. She would give away her last farthing BUT, if anyone was to perform a mean trick or try to take advantage of her, they would find in Marie Goossens a formidable and relentless adversary. As Léon would say, his sister was a marvellous girl, far too good for this world and, unlike the boys, *never* did anything wrong!

Next came Adolphe, so soon to be cut off in his prime. Although quiet by nature, he was a very strong young man, full of charm and poise, and it was he who invariably fought Léon's battles. He could also be wicked. One day the family were sitting at Sunday lunch when shouts from the street and the imminent arrival of the horse-drawn fire brigade led them to realise that one of their upper rooms was ablaze. In a matter of seconds, there was great confusion as the lumbering firemen created a human chain to send buckets of water to the seat of the fire.

Annie Goossens was wailing, "Don't let the water ruin my carpets" while the boys were intent upon becoming part of the bucket platoon. Their efforts infuriated one of the firemen, who promptly locked them in a room, but Adolphe contrived to escape and, ·leading out his brothers, they inserted themselves alongside the firemen. When Adolphe received his first pail of water, he promptly discharged it over the head of the obnoxious fireman below. It was rumoured, dare it be reported, that Adolphe had a fondness for matches, but somehow the culprit was never quite tied down!

Next around the table was Léon, the baby among the boys, not too good at fending for himself in the rough outside Liverpudlian world, but ably protected by his brothers; mischievous to a degree, full of fun and sharing with Eugène a love for trains and things mechanical. Lastly came little Sidonie.

Decorative and delightful; all the family adored Sid. Having started to play the violin, she one day heard a passing fire engine and, tumbling down the stairs in her excitement, broke her collar bone and was later unable to hold her instrument with ease. She decided to join Marie, who was already well advanced in playing the harp.

Both girls in later life were to meet personal tragedy. Marie was to marry Frederick Lawrence, manager of the

and Eugène, in his encouraging manner as elder brother, proceeded to put Léon through his paces. He accompanied all the oboe items before the concert proper began, and gave Léon invaluable hints and advice.

They commenced playing, Eugène upon the violin, Adolphe the French horn and Léon the oboe, and thereby the third generation of Goossens started upon their not inconsiderable professional careers with the *William Tell* Overture.

Somehow this début marked the transition between adolescence and teenage manhood for, only a few weeks previously, as is the habit with the young male animal, Léon and Adolphe had been scrapping. Normally they were the best of pals but, upon this day, they so aggravated one another that they fought like dogs.

Léon had upset Adolphe, who was giving him a ride in his wheelbarrow. Apparently goaded to the point of exasperation, the young horn player commenced a suicidally fast run down the garden path, with the aspiring oboist clinging on for dear life. Straight at the closed french windows he aimed and, with an almighty shattering of glass, they landed in the sitting-room. Poor Mum was in the kitchen at the moment of impact, but not for long! Frightened out of her life and wondering what on earth had happened, she came storming into the room. Two very chastened young musicians were soundly beaten and sent to their beds, as well they deserved.

At this time, Eugène had just taken his Oxford Local Examination in furtherance of his normal scholastic career. He passed all subjects well, with the notable exception of music!

Duly fortified, for he disliked school intensely, he appealed to his father that he should be allowed to enter for the "Liverpool" Scholarship to the Royal College of Music. This was a much coveted competition and, in due course, escorted by Papa, Eugène journeyed by train and horse-bus to London for the examination.

Among the musical judiciary were Sir Hubert Parry, Director of the College, Sir Charles Stanford, Sir Frederick Bridge, Sir Walter Parratt, E. Fernandez Arbós, Achille Rivarde and W. E. Whitehouse. This stern array of masters was sufficient to intimidate any young aspiring student, but throughout the day youngsters from all over the country competed with tense expectancy.

Eugène began with the Mendelssohn Concerto and then followed with an unaccompanied prelude and fugue from a Bach sonata. Having been thanked for the effort, the young violinist was dismissed and spent interminable hours with his father, whiling away the time as the other competitors were heard. All the young players, escorted by their parents, were forced to wait in a large uncomfortable room and, as the day drew to a close, it was a somewhat incredulous Eugène who was approached by Frank Pownall, the Registrar of the college, who said to him, "Congratulations, young man, you did splendidly." It was a rewarding moment for father and son alike.

That summer, before the autumn term began, Eugène Goossens the Second and his wife took the family to Llandudno for a holiday. They journeyed as usual by paddle-steamer, devouring masses of egg and chicken sandwiches, for somehow it was apparent to all, both parents and children alike, that the family were now entering upon a new and exciting phase in their young lives.

It was shortly after this vacation that Thomas Beecham came to Liverpool as guest conductor with the Philharmonic Orchestra. A third oboe was urgently required and young Léon was engaged. Upon arrival for rehearsal, Beecham could not resist a quip, and referring to the Child Performance Regulations rejoined, "I trust our third oboist has a licence!"

In early 1912 Eugène Goossens II decided that the time had now come for the family to return to London. His eldest son had already spent two years at the Royal College and, although Adolphe and Léon were too young to enter a scholarship competition, nevertheless he decided that they should join their brother at that institution without further delay.

Thus, at the age of fourteen, Léon completed his normal scholastic education and transferred his full time attention to the world of music.

Prior to their departure to the south, the family had taken a holiday to attend the Brussels Exhibition. The fact that a day or two later it was burnt to the ground did not prevent the blame for this catastrophe descending upon the shoulders of young Adolphe for, as will be recalled, he enjoyed a certain reputation for starting conflagrations!

During the two years that Eugène had been studying alone in London, joined in the winter by his father when conducting seasons of Carl Rosa at Covent Garden, he had lodged at the establishment of one Miss Fanny Lynch. This tiny Irish lady of some sixty years or so, was a leading member of the Suffragette Movement. She had recently moved her residence from Cromwell Road to the heights of Campden Hill, where she acquired an address in Berkeley Gardens. It was lavishly decorated with the purple and green flags of her Movement, and Papa Goossens arranged that after the spring vacation young Eugène would escort Marie and his two young brothers to Miss Lynch's household for a period of two weeks, while he and his wife, retaining Sidonie, would supervise the big move to 70 Edith Road, West Kensington.

At that period there was an experimental express which left Liverpool at 4.5, dashing to London in not much more time than the new diesel locomotives. The boys were train-mad and Léon had always been mechanically minded. It

E

was, therefore, in a high pitch of feverish excitement that the young travellers loaded up one of White's broughams for the very last time. Father's and grandfather's leather cases were pressed into service and were hauled atop the cab to accompany the children.

Young Eugène assumed all the importance of his position as eldest son, while Marie responded with maternal care for her two younger brothers. The main line station at Liverpool bustled with activity as the giant locomotives belched forth steam with whistles shrilling and porters scurrying between the groups of departing passengers. Léon was wide-eyed with excitement and clutching his sandwiches, was shortly established in a corner seat, wiping away but a single tear at the prospect of leaving behind his dear mother and father.

With a last satisfying gulp of steam and smoke enveloping the platform, the 4.5 p.m. began its important journey southward, eventually arriving dead on the dot at Euston Station. Eugène, a worldly and much travelled young gentleman, held the tickets and, ushering his charges through the barrier, struggled to keep them together as they entered upon yet another new wonder of technical achievement— the Underground railway. Léon was entranced as much as his sister was alarmed!

The young family were swiftly conveyed to Notting Hill Gate station and emerged from one mechanical marvel to observe, on this delightful spring evening, many more. Léon's memory of this moment remains undimmed. The first thing he noticed was the surface of the road. Unlike Liverpool the granite sets had given way to wooden blocks, tarmacadamed all over and which, due to the passage of the traffic, had been polished to a shiny, ebony black. Then he saw the solid-tyred De Dion-Bouton buses jostling aside the many horse-drawn cabs. There was an odd taxi or two and, another innovation, the steam-driven bus.

With eyes filled with wonder, young Léon allowed himself

to be chivvied into a cab and, shortly, the exhilarated young family were making the acquaintance of dear Miss Lynch. After a light supper they were taken to the attic where their beds awaited them and, prior to falling asleep, Léon listened to a meeting being held below with the object of furthering the Suffragettes Movement and obtaining the vote for women. It had been an exciting day.

Some two weeks later the family were reunited in Edith Road and, as he entered the house, the first thing that struck the observant eye of young Léon was the electric wire which travelled across the ceiling and ended in a light bulb. This innovation was a vast improvement upon the Liverpudlian gas mantle to which they were so accustomed. But, with Grandfather's Bechstein grand comfortably standing in the music room, the transition from the north to the south was smooth and complete. In the matter of a day or two Léon, his two brothers and his sister would commence term at the Royal College of Music.

Upon that auspicious early summer morning, Eugène the Third led his fraternal young protégés down Church Street, Kensington, past the Carmelite church, with the spire of St. Mary Abbots in the distance, into Kensington Gardens, past the Palace, over the Broad Walk, until they came to the Round Pond. Here he had difficulty in dragging the youngest member of the party away from the water's edge where already local enthusiasts were launching their barques and square-rigged schooners which would take part in races far more exciting than the Grain Run to Sydney.

In a fit of exasperation, Zen called out, "Come on, Lee, we can't be late on the first morning," and so, with this admonishment ringing in their ears, the little cavalcade moved forward.

Léon was duly impressed, if a little nervous, as he mounted the steps to the College. They were ushered into the Principal's office and Eugène politely introduced each of them to

Sir Hubert Parry. He was a most endearing old gentleman and seemed delighted with the new infusion of Goossens' blood.

It was explained to Léon that his professor for the oboe would be Malsch, who was principal oboist with one of the big London orchestras, and that he would also be taking piano as a second instrument, with harmony.

So began two happy years at the College, where discipline was strict, especially with regard to segregation of the sexes, but where much good work was done. Life settled down to a routine, divided equally between the five-bedroomed house in Edith Road, which Léon's father rented for the princely sum of £60 a year, and the R.C.M.

Within a short time of arrival the sound of piano playing from the neighbour next door proclaimed the presence of another young pianist. The house was occupied by a jolly well-proportioned French lady with her young daughter, whose name, it transpired, was Yvonne Arnaud. They kept a flock of chickens in the garden and both families became firm friends.

At the beginning of each week, Léon was given half a crown to cover his expenses for five days at College. 1d. each way for the bus if he so desired, 2d. for lunchtime soup, and 2d. for dessert, which usually consisted of treacle tart. With four children it was impossible to run to a main course.

The Royal College of Music has changed little in the last sixty or seventy years, except perhaps for the cost of meals! There is still the foyer with the central staircase but, in Léon's day, only boys were permitted to mount on the left-hand side because the girls demurely ascended on the right. Although they came together in the concert hall and for tuition, little fraternisation was allowed. The austere Mrs. Bindon governed the girls like a hawk stooping on a flock of doves, and on one occasion when Léon had the temerity to hold conversation with a member of the opposite sex mount-

ing the far side of the staircase, he received a severe lecture
and reprimand. It was not until Mrs. Bindon had exhausted
her carefully chosen phrases on the evil of sex too-young-in-
life that Léon was able to assure that good lady that he was
only talking to his sister!

By this time Zen had reached such lofty heights within the
College that he was promoted to the leadership of the second
violins. However, his new-found status was to receive a
severe knock, as he modestly recounted many years later,
when Saint-Saëns was invited to conduct a rehearsal of his
Third Symphony with the school orchestra.

All went well until the finale, when the second violins
bungled a lead; Saint-Saëns turned to Eugène's section, and,
with the withering look of scorn he sometimes affected,
addressed them in French; "Play that by yourselves, second
violins." They did, horribly. He looked at Zen. "You. Show
the others how it should go." He did, tremulously and
ineffectively. Saint-Saëns glared for what seemed ages. Then
he removed his pince-nez and apostrophised: "Gentil garcon,
mais quel sacre violiniste!" (Nice boy, but what an awful
violinist!) Then, to the orchestra (pointing to Eugène)
"Vairy nervose . . .!" and they proceeded, but for the rest of
the rehearsal Eugène felt crushed and humiliated. When the
rehearsal ended, and Saint-Saëns turned to leave the ros-
trum, the young orchestra stood up. At that moment the
great man caught Zen's eye and—winked!

*   *   *

These years saw the emergence and recognition of men
such as Thomas Beecham, Henry Wood and in the world of
ballet the young Massine, who came straight from the Ballet
School of the Imperial Theatre in Moscow. There were so
many legendary figures at that time; Nijinsky, Fokine, Bolm,
Pavlova, Karsavina and the master, Cechetti. Diaghilev had
just commissioned the young Stravinsky to carry out a new

opera experience which resulted in the production of the legendary *Firebird*.

Léon's father was still conducting the Carl Rosa and, on the morning following the opening night's *Tannhauser*, the family were extremely proud that their entirely modest parent received the lion's share of the press notices.

It was not long before the young fourteen-year-old Léon Goossens duly impressed his professors at the Royal College. Likewise his brother Adolphe showed amazing mastery of the French horn. The first solo piece that Léon learned under Malsch was Handel's Sonata No. 1 for Oboe. It is an exquisite piece of music and it was the thought, brought home to him in Malta, that he might never again be able to play such work, that occasioned him his agony of mind.

*   *   *

One jet-black night, standing with Leslie, silent beside the gently lapping waves of the Mediterranean, he heard in the music vault of his mind Bach's solo piece for the oboe in the *Easter Oratorio*. It depicts the arrival of the Apostles at the sepulchre and they find that the body of their Lord is no longer contained within. The feeling of devastation and despair is overwhelming. The composer selected the oboe to convey this haunting mood and it summed up, in all its futility, the present plight of Léon Goossens.

9

The Great War

AFTER APPROXIMATELY six weeks in the early autumn sunshine of the George Cross island, the outward physical repair
of Léon would seem to the casual observer to be complete.
The weather was breaking and an inevitable return to
London had to be faced.

Already the legal ramifications of the accident were beginning to impinge on their lazy days, and so on a clear autumn
morning, Léon and his wife, having taken a most grateful
farewell of their friends, especially the Royal Navy dental
surgeon, found themselves sitting comfortably aboard an
aircraft bound for England. It was not long before they saw
the alpine peaks below, jagged and remorseless, bearing the
first white mantle of autumnal snow as gradually they made
their way northward across France, a France that Léon
Goossens had known only too well, *circa* 1915–18.

In 1914, having completed two years at the Royal College
of Music, Léon's father was approached by that institution
and asked whether or not he would wish his son to enter for
the woodwind scholarship, having now attained the eligible
age of sixteen. It was with a wry sense of fun that Eugène the
Second declined the offer, pointing out that it would have
proved most acceptable two years previously!

Then, suddenly, a week following the grand season of

Russian ballet and opera at Drury Lane Theatre, conducted by the young Thomas Beecham with three new ballets specially commissioned by Diaghilev, Great Britain declared war upon Germany. There was a giddy sense of elation amongst the younger generation, little realising the holocaust that lay before them.

In a fit of patriotic fervour, led by Zen, the three young brothers endeavoured to enlist in the Officers' Training Corps. Somewhat crestfallen they were informed that not only were Léon and Adolphe too young, but that Eugène was not robust enough to pass his medical. In any case, as they had not been to public schools, they would not be eligible as potential officer material! However, it was not very long before their country would have need of them!

In the meantime, Eugène who had left the College amidst great approbation, managed to secure for himself a place in the Queen's Hall Orchestra under the baton of Henry Wood. Summer came creeping over an unsuspecting England and following the Earl's Court Exhibition, the season of Promenade Concerts began at the Queen's Hall.

At last came Léon's chance to hear the renowned oboist, Henri du Busscher. Zen now occupied his place among the violins, behind the potted palms, and his younger brother Lee joined the sea of eager upturned faces, duly assembled punctually at eight, to listen to whatever was offered them.

At the first concert du Busscher played two works, the lovely solo in the Good Friday music by Wagner and the Strauss tone poem, *Don Juan*. The young oboist listened entranced to an undoubted master. It was just what he needed. Here was a player even superior to the Belgian oboist in his father's orchestra who had first inspired him as a child. Du Busscher's tone was mellow and beautifully disciplined. He was undoubtedly the finest oboist that the young student had ever heard. In a way it was an unsettling experience for the young musician, who did not believe that he was

ABOVE : A typical Belgian
family one might say.
Eugène Goossens II, his wife
Annie Cook, their son Léon
and granddaughters.

RIGHT : Léon's distinguished
and dearly loved father.

RIGHT : Newly wed on a roof top in Chelsea. Dancer Leslie Burrowes; young oboist Léon Goossens.

BELOW : Leslie Burrowes dancing 'Pastorale Lunaire'.

capable of reaching such perfection. Little did he know that not many months hence he was to be offered the opportunity of replacing du Busscher, who was to resign in the spring of 1915 to take up an excellent position with the Los Angeles Philharmonic Orchestra.

Back at college Léon continued his studies under Sir Charles Stanford, who conducted the student orchestra, perched high up on a stool, his old pipe drooping from his lips, his pince-nez askew upon his nose. "Keep awake, m'boy," he would constantly admonish. Léon learnt much from the old master, especially the reading of Brahms, for Sir Charles had been alive in that composer's lifetime.

*   *   *

With a glowing report written by Sir Hubert Parry, Léon's days at the R.C.M. came to an end, and coincided one night with the arrival home in Edith Road of an highly excited Eugène.

"Where's Lee?" he exclaimed, bubbling over. "I have some tremendous news; du Busscher is leaving the orchestra to go to America. I have suggested that Léon could possibly replace him!"

As it happened his younger brother had already been introduced to several members of the orchestra, including the charming Frederick Kiddle, whose additional task in life was to accompany solo artists on the piano. Of course, the whole thing was quite preposterous. Principal oboists were men seldom beneath the age of forty, but Eugène had the greatest faith in his brother and was always full of encouragement, never failing to broadcast the talent being nurtured at the College.

Mr. Newman, Sir Henry's manager, undoubtedly spoke to Sir Hubert, and in due course a highly nervous Léon was summoned to an audition. He was to present himself at the Queen's Hall on a Sunday afternoon in the late summer, together with a piece of music of his choosing. He would be auditioned by Sir Henry, following the afternoon concert. Father Goossens noticed, with some apprehension, the nervousness of his youngest son and endeavoured to bolster his courage.

On the appointed day it was agreed that Léon should go to the Queen's Hall alone, and immediately following the concert, Eugène would meet him and make the necessary introductions. After all, his eldest brother was now all of twenty-one!

At last the hour arrived and, armed with a concerto by Colin, the French composer, who had written the piece for a competition, Léon timorously and well before time, presented himself at the side door of the old Queen's Hall. He gained access and found himself standing in a passageway with only a door between himself and the French horns. The orchestra were coming to the triumphant finale of the 1812. The church bells were ringing and the cannons were firing to such an extent that, for a moment, Léon forgot his nervousness, caught up in the exhilaration of the music. Of a sudden the concert had ended, the roars of applause had died away, and Eugène appeared miraculously at his elbow.

"Come on, Lee, don't be nervous. Good luck," and with these comforting words, Léon Goossens found himself walking upon the stage.

He was immensely relieved to see the person of Frederick Kiddle, who extended a kindly welcome, whispering:

"Jolly good luck. I don't think you need worry about this."

Immediately Léon felt more calm, for Kiddle had heard him play upon another occasion.

Suddenly a side door in the auditorium opened and Sir Henry made his entrance in a heavy fur-lined coat, looking extremely warm, having only just completed the afternoon's conducting. As usual he sported a white buttonhole in his lapel, the flower kept alive in the heat by the minute phial of water in which it rested.

"Good afternoon, Mr. Goossens," he called, and coming forward reached up his delicately boned hand. "This is Mr.

Newman," he said, indicating his manager at his side, "Now, what are we going to hear?"

"A little piece by Colin," Léon stammered, and retreated from the great man's presence to the centre of the platform. Eugène was not to be seen, but Léon knew that he would be standing concealed at the side. Suddenly taking hold of himself, he found his composure and, moistening his lips and reed, he turned to Kiddle. He nodded, and that gentleman smiled his encouragement in return.

It was a flowery piece and Léon took it in his stride, but this was only the beginning. Age had no part in such an audition. He was not being called upon to compete for a second position, but for principal oboist. They tested his sight reading; a sheet of music was placed before him. It was Brahms. Everything that Sir Charles Stanford had taught him came to Léon's aid. He looked at it coolly, raised the reed to his lips, and began to play. The very act of performing gave him ever-increasing confidence, until suddenly, in the middle of the piece, his eye was distracted for a brief second by a movement up in the gallery. One glance was sufficient and he became petrified, his self-assurance stripped away. There stood the man who knew everything, far more frightening than a hundred Sir Henry Woods! It was his dear father, dressed for the street with his malacca cane. Léon's knees turned to jelly but, in the next second, the piano having carried the melody, his turn came again. Now he was petrified but fighting to master his fear, he continued and finally brought the piece to its gentle conclusion.

"Very good, very good indeed," came the voice floating up from the stalls. "Just one more, if you don't mind," and Léon duly obliged.

It is said that Wood admitted to being thoroughly amazed at the young man's virtuosity. Walking forward he thanked Léon, concluding with that evergreen phrase, "You will be hearing from us, Mr. Goossens."

The anti-climax was horrible, but the day's work had been well done, and Papa Goossens with his eldest son, escorted young Léon home.

*   *   *

But it was not that simple to become principal oboist of the famous Queen's Hall Orchestra. A letter did arrive and most gratifying it was to receive.

Mr. Newman, the manager, informed Léon that the orchestra was shortly to undertake a ten-day tour of Wales and they would be very delighted if he would care to accompany them as principal oboist. This was tremendously exciting, but the young musician was filled with self-doubt. How could he possibly, so soon after emerging from college, be expected to compete with veterans upon the concert platform? He discussed it at length with his father and, much to the chagrin of Zen, wrote back to Mr. Newman that he considered his experience insufficient and, much as he would have loved to have taken part, he felt that he must reluctantly decline.

But to the considerable credit of Sir Henry and the management, they decided to press the matter further. There is no doubt that they had an eye upon the future. The early signs were clear. With guidance and orchestral experience they believed that they would find in the young musician a man to replace Henri du Busscher.

And so, formally attired and diffidently carrying his instrument, Léon took his place among the orchestra for the first concert of the tour.

When the ten-day engagement came to an end, Léon returned home and for four months heard no more. Indeed he believed, in spite of assurances from his brother, that the tour must have proved a disaster. However, when du Busscher departed just before the summer season of Proms, a second letter arrived from Mr. Newman. The post of princi-

pal oboist at the Queen's Hall was offered and accepted by
Léon Goossens at the age of seventeen.

It was an exhilarating and demanding task thrust upon
such young shoulders, and Léon made his fair share of errors,
but he was learning with remarkable speed. His brother
Zen recalled, "Sitting in the same orchestra with Léon, I
remember marvelling at his sang-froid and musicianship
when, confronted by a succession of new works (many un-
rehearsed) he would give an immaculate account of all of
them. Knowing the repertory, I always anticipated with
some trepidation his first encounter with the oboistic high
spots of the standard orchestral literature: things like the slow
movement from the Brahm's Violin Concerto, the cadenza at
the opening of the Beethoven Fifth, the second Brandenburg
Concerto, and the obligati from the Bach arias, not to mention
the difficult passages of Strauss, Debussy and Sibelius."

It is natural that the recollection of the first night of the
promenade season remains vividly in Léon's mind. Upon
countless occasions he had been in the audience at these
concerts, and now he was himself to perform. Being a
principal he had to make a personal entrance upon the
platform and received, as did his colleagues, his own round
of applause. It must have been a unique sight for the
promenaders and also for his parents and family, who were
undoubtedly tingling with excitement in the audience below.

Petrified though he was, Léon performed immaculately. Sir
Henry was a tower of strength and indeed throughout the entire
season, treated his young protégé with tireless consideration.

After the performance, Léon and his brother celebrated
in the milk-bar alongside Oxford Circus station. It was some
weeks later, very close to the same spot, that the young oboist
saw the silvery arms of the searchlights pick out the Wellsian,
cigar-shaped Zeppelin. It was cruising leisurely at some
5,000 feet or so, eventually turning north where it was shot
down in spectacular fashion by early fighter pilot Captain

Robinson over Cuffley in Herts. This brought the war very near, and, with another birthday looming, a call to arms.

Adolphe had months before laid aside his French horn and enlisted in the Artists' Rifles. Upon joining, the regiment were encamped in Richmond Park, but then moved to High Beech in Epping Forest. Consequently Adolphe managed to pop home for the odd week-end or evening meal, and on one such occasion he was in danger of missing the last bus north. Léon pulled out his push-bike, encouraged his brother to leap upon the step, and pedalled furiously to the Addison Bridge bus stop. As they reached it in the nick of time, Adolphe called over his shoulder "Don't stop, I'll just hop off. Thanks Lee. Goodbye," and without even a backward glance, Léon pedalled home, never to see his brother again.

Léon attempted through an introduction to become a Royal Naval Air Service pilot, but his attempts were frustrated, and he finally joined the Middlesex Yeomanry. He was stationed in Arbour Hill Barracks in Dublin, breaking and schooling horses for the Western Front. One black night while he was on guard, a telegram was handed to him. It read simply:

"TRAGIC NEWS. POOR ADIE DIED OF WOUNDS YESTERDAY. DAD."

Léon was shattered. He was relieved of his duties but only reached the guardroom before he broke down. Poor, dear Adolphe. His parents and his family were distraught and from that time Papa Goossens never smoked a cigar or pipe again.

Léon was made up to lance-corporal, and had a bosom pal named Gearing. They suddenly found they could no longer stomach their secure occupation in Dublin, and decided to join the infantry. Losses in the British Army had been mounting to such severe proportions that volunteers were urgently required. Thus, without knowing it, Léon was embarking upon the first step in a near fatal cycle of events, closely following upon that of his late brother. He and his friend found themselves in the 8th Royal Fusiliers, 12th Division—the "Ace of Spades" and so shortly started training at Etaples, France.

It was at this time that he learned the way of Adolphe's going. There had been severe casualties, and men in the Artists' Rifles gained for themselves the distinction of becoming officer-producing units. The calibre of the individuals was so high, all being volunteers, that upon request, the private soldiers agreed to be commissioned in the field, and placing their new badges of rank upon their epaulettes, assumed command of platoons up and down the front line.

The very next morning, with a sergeant who boasted that he had never yet brought back an officer alive, Adolphe went into the attack. Eyewitnesses said that he was somewhat carried away and, rushing forward, reached the parapet of the forward German trench all alone. He was cut down by murderous fire.

The following day a Roman Catholic priest, who had known him, heard of the incident and immediately cycled up to that section of the front. Leaving his bicycle he proceeded forward unescorted and, amazingly, amidst the carnage of no-man's-land, he came upon Adolphe, still alive but dying. He had been hit by an explosive bullet, and it was a miracle that he still survived some twenty-four hours later. The dedicated priest administered the last rites, and stayed with Adolphe until he died.

Then came Léon's turn, as his unit moved into the line. He had spent many devastating months in the trenches and on April 9, 1917, took part in the battle of Arras. Preceding it was the heaviest barrage ever to be laid down in the first world war. The guns stood wheel to wheel, and our troops advanced behind a veritable blanket of shells. Following the action, once again the call went up for more officer volunteers and Léon decided, under pressure, that he must return to England for training and to take his commission—public school or no public school!

His mother was particularly distraught when she learned of Léon's intention, for the prospect of yet another son becoming a second lieutenant with a life expectancy of only a few weeks filled her with foreboding. Strangely, up until this point, Léon had been quite sure that he would survive, certainly while serving in the ranks. His religious belief was so strong that he knew nothing would happen, but the significance of the step he had now taken did not escape him, and not unnaturally he viewed the future with something less than optimism.

*   *   *

Before joining up he had placed his oboe in the Midland Bank in Pall Mall, and there it was to remain, for three long years. Music had hardly occupied his thoughts during the last few years, but while he had been billeted in Arras, or rather living in the caves beneath the Grand Place, Léon had been approached to play the harmonium in the ruined Pro-Cathedral in which Sunday services were held. The piano having been his second instrument, the young lance-corporal had been able to achieve a reasonable performance, practising beforehand and noting in his soldiers' prayer book the points at which he should manipulate the stops in order to gain some light and shade from the large harmonium.

While in the church he felt a certain security, an uplifting of the soul, which was in violent contrast to his emotions in the front line. On one day in particular, May 3, 1917, during his previous time in the trenches, he had gone over the top three times before darkness fell, and on another he and Gearing had actually witnessed something which had been rumoured many times; a German machine gunner chained to his weapon. The poor fellow had lost part of his face and was not yet dead. He sat huddled with his hands in his pockets, enough reason being left within his torn frame to try to keep warm. It was merciful to end his misery.

Somehow there was an inexplicable gulf between the harmonium in the Pro-Cathedral and the horror in the front line a few hundred yards away.

10

Commissioned

BACK IN ENGLAND with its desperate attempt at gaiety, patriotism still ran high, although the country had become drab and war weary. Léon was sent to No. 3 Officer Training Battalion at Parkhurst in the Isle of Wight, and some six months later was posted, duly commissioned, to the regimental depot of the Sherwood Foresters in Nottingham.

It has to be recorded that relations between the new single-pipper and his Commanding Officer were by no means serene. It was generally known in the Mess that Léon could play the piano, but unfortunately the Colonel did not have a musical ear. Consequently the strains of "If You Were The Only Girl In The World" that echoed through the passages and rooms in the Officers' Mess only infuriated the C.O. further, until Léon, returning from leave in London, found his name at the head of a list of half a dozen officers who were urgently required to reinforce a battalion on the Western Front.

With a few days extra embarkation leave, Léon hurried to London. It so happened that a little time previously his brother, Eugène, had conducted a new opera *The Bosun's Mate* by Ethel Smyth. She had been so entranced that she had given him a silver cigarette case, and now Zen, being moved by a sudden inspiration, decided to pass it on to his younger brother.

F

"Here, Lee, you take this with you. I never use it and I'm sure Ethel Smyth would be delighted if I gave it to you."

Léon was equally pleased to accept it, and he placed it alongside his steel shaving mirror in the left breast pocket of his tunic. A few hours later he was well on the way to France.

It was the first week of November 1918, but little did Léon realise that within ten days the war would be over. However, it was not to be soon enough for him.

He arrived aboard a truck under cover of darkness on November 3 at Landrecies on the Somme.

Having almost reached their destination, they heard a shell whistling down towards them. They hurled themselves over the tailboard, the shell exploding some fifty yards in front. Scrambling to his feet, the driver pointed forward in the darkness. "There's no need for me to go any farther, it's just a few yards up the road!"

They were shortly being received by their new colonel. "Jolly nice to see you chaps. You're just in time. We're putting in a major attack the day after tomorrow."

Léon managed a weak grin. He had been over the top too many times to harbour any sense of occasion, and being tired, he felt quite ill at the prospect. Next he was taken to meet his new company commander, who was equally enthusiastic. "So you've arrived. Good show. You've just got time for a few hours sleep because I'd like you to take out a patrol in the morning. I'll introduce you to your platoon; they are expecting you."

Léon's morale was not high, and it was shortly to be lowered still farther.

"Your platoon sergeant," the company commander said. "This is Mr. Goossens."

There was a faint look of surprise and semi-recognition from this veteran. "I was your brother's platoon sergeant in the Norfolks, sir. I was with him on the day he died."

This was the man who boasted that he had never brought back an officer alive!

He was assigned a batman whose name was White and who had made up a bed upon which he shortly fell asleep from sheer exhaustion. Before daybreak and stand-to, he received his first instructions. It was to probe forward, taking just a couple of men, to see if they could locate the German positions. The battle line had moved from the trenches and was now somewhat more mobile. There was a cemetery in front of them and beyond it an old farmhouse. The corporal Léon took with him suggested they should investigate the building. With the third man weighed down with a machine-gun, the trio moved forward. It was deadly still on a cold autumn morning, the silence occasionally broken by the explosion of a solitary shell. No birds were singing.

After much crawling they neared the farmhouse and saw a white flag displayed. Satisfying themselves that it was not occupied by the enemy, they drew closer and noticed heavy wooden trap doors obviously covering a cellar. They decided to open them and were amazed at the sight that met their eyes. There was an entire French family gathered together around the bedside of their dying grandmother. The cellar was white and clean, and candles burnt in niches. The old grand dame looked perfectly serene and the faces of the family were even happy, for they realised that British troops were gradually advancing, throwing out the detested Boche.

Léon handed down some cigarettes and chocolate, closed the wooden doors and moved on forward. Suddenly they noticed some grey-clad figures behind a hedge at 200 yards range, and saw a platoon of German soldiery stamping on the ground to keep warm. Without a moment's hesitation, they found a suitable position and set up the machine-gun. Seconds later they opened fire. To their amazement the Germans hurled down their weapons and came racing towards them, hands held high. Only their officer tried a movement of treachery, and the machine-gunner cut him down. On Léon's first day as an officer on active service, he had unwittingly captured an entire enemy platoon.

The German officer had been carrying two automatics, one a Mauser with a beautiful wooden holster. These Léon commandeered, but not for long. Events seemed to be moving ever more quickly, almost as if it were beyond his control.

That evening the colonel was busy selecting the names of the officers who would lead the attack on the following morning. At the end of his deliberations he was left with two second-lieutenants, of whom he only needed one. There were rueful smiles on the faces of the officers and the colonel, laughing, who said, "You'd better toss for it." He extracted a coin from his pocket and sent it spinning high in the air. "Call, Goossens," he ordered. "Tails, sir." The jovial O.C. snatched it from the air and flicked it on to the back of his hand.

"Heads," he declared. "Congratulations, Goossens, you're on."

Amid the general amusement Léon felt somewhat queasy. However, the low ebb of his morale was to be dropped a point or two farther by the action of the battalion M.O. He had been sitting at a trestle table in the corner, busily writing the names of the officers on labels, so that they would be conveniently to hand in the event of their becoming casualties. Turning to Léon, he said cheerfully, "I say, what's your name, old man? I had better make one out for you as you're going!"

"Goossens." The twenty-one-year-old second-lieutenant replied formally. In the event it would be the first label to be used.

Léon retired for a few hours rest, weary in body and mind, instructing White, his batman, to call him at 4 a.m. As he lay awake he contemplated the situation and could not keep the image of Adolphe out of his mind. He prayed for the sake of his family that he also would not be killed. He thought of Eugène and Henry Wood at home. Even Sir Henry was a member of the G.R.—General Reserve—known affectionately to one and all as "God's Refuse".

Everyone now seemed embroiled in the war, but there was a general air of optimism. At long last the Hun was being smashed, but it had taken a long time adoing, and not without the inestimable help of our American allies. Léon was reminded of one of the few elevating sights that he had seen during the entire war. It was the parade ground near Etaples known as the Bull Ring. Here each morning on a vast expanse of barrack square, representative troops from every regiment in the British Army paraded with their colours. There were Indians, Gurkhas, the Home Regiments, the Australians, New Zealanders, Canadians and South Africans, all of them polished to a pitch of near perfection. It was as if the whole free world had taken up arms against a vile oppressor. The following morning at day-break Léon would become victim to one tiny move as a pawn in the less glorious side of the game.

He said his prayers and tossed and turned in shallow sleep. It seemed that he had no sooner closed his eyes than a hand was tugging at his shoulder. The unfamiliar face of White handed him a mug of tea.

"It's 4 a.m., sir."

"Oh, thanks," Goossens replied sleepily.

He was shortly preparing for battle in that cold and friendless hour, commonly hated by all infantrymen. Léon decided to wear an extra cardigan. It was canary yellow in colour, although shortly to be stained a different hue. He was determined to be warm, for his one dread thought throughout his front line experience was ever to be seen to be afraid. Everyone without exception was tormented with fear, but each man tried in his individual way to conceal it. This would be his first attack as an officer leading his own men. The cold autumn pre-dawn air must not make him shiver.

He put on his tunic, boots and gaiters, spun the well oiled chamber of his ·45 Colt revolver and slipped in six rounds. He could feel his stomach fluttering; downing a hot mug of tea and forcing himself to eat a corned beef sandwich, he felt a little better.

He moved with his platoon to their position. They were lying some way short of the graveyard when the barrage began. No trenches this time, but an advance over open ground. Of a sudden the battle erupted and having advanced a short way, they were soon pinned down. They had reached within forty yards of the enemy when a man on his left was hit by a bullet, which curved down his spine. He was screaming. Almost in the same instant the platoon commander on his right was killed. It would have been suicide to press forward, but something had to be done. As usual there was chaos, confusion and noise. To the right ran a road some few yards away, and straddling it were our own machine-gunners.

A flanking movement might help, momentarily appraised the young lieutenant. What the hell was going on to the right? With a shouted word to his sergeant, he leapt to his feet and ran hard towards the road, covering the intervening space in a matter of seconds. As he reached the machine-gunners he hurled himself down. As luck would have it, he found himself beside another officer, still unharmed.

"What are you going to do?" he shouted the question above the cacophony of sound.

Even before he received a reply, he felt a strange force pushing him back across the ground. In surprise and shock he glanced down towards the breast pocket of his tunic. It was torn. The high velocity machine-gun bullet at a mere forty yards range had hit him a fraction above the heart. He could see his yellow cardigan slowly staining red. There was no pain. He turned to the officer.

"I've had it," he said simply.

"O.K.!" came the reply, "don't try to move."

Within seconds the stretcher bearers arrived, and so did White, his batman, crawling across the intervening ground as the attack crept forward. His eyes lighted on Léon's captured German automatics.

"You won't need those where you're going. I'll bring them back with the rest of your kit, sir."

It was the last Léon ever saw of his batman, or indeed his spoils of war!

Amid the sounds of battle and the ever increasing daylight, Léon Goossens was transferred to the rear, shortly to find himself at a forward dressing station. The M.O. was ready with his label. An orderly broke four needles while injecting him for tetanus. The surgeon began to examine him.

"How do you feel?"

"A bit numb."

"You're damned lucky, old man," he countered, taking out from Léon's pocket the steel shaving mirror and Zen's cigarette case. A bullet had pierced clean through the mirror, had reached the soft metal of the cigarette case, and been deflected down, cutting a comparatively superficial furrow across his ribs, and then out into the cold French soil.

"They saved your life, Goossens," the M.O. exclaimed, replacing the objects in Léon's other pocket. "It will have to be stitched and cauterised." He then placed a large "B" on the label.

"What's that mean?"

"A Blighty one, you lucky dog."

Léon managed a smile.

It was November 5. On the 9th his parents received another telegram at Edith Road; on the 10th he reached

Epsom War Hospital and on November 11 the 1918 war ended.

*   *   *

Léon looked down at the sand dunes of northern France, saw the cold grey English Channel, choppy under the lash of an autumn breeze. It would not be long before their aircraft landed at London Airport. And then what? He sighed.

*   *   *

He would never forget the scene when his mother and father visited him on the day he reached Epsom Hospital. He was having a bed bath when they arrived and screens were drawn round him. He could hear his dearly loved Mum before he could see her! She had obviously cried all the way, but it was nothing to her reaction when she saw the screens! She jumped to a premature conclusion, believing that Léon was about to depart this world. Pushing them aside, a mischievous son endeavoured to reassure his mother that he was still very much alive. Poor Dad looked gaunt and grey, although much relieved at the cheerful countenance that confronted him. They were still both in mourning for Adolphe.

The following day the hospital was paralysed by the ecstatic news that the Armistice had been signed. Bed cases were out when they shouldn't have been, white starched nurses were almost disrobed in wild elation. But Léon would not obtain his discharge from the hospital until December 27, two long months away.

*   *   *

There was a sudden jolt as the aircraft wheels locked down, which had the useful effect of bringing Léon back to the present. Suddenly they were poised above the edge of the tarmac, and, turning to Leslie, Léon smiled. Twenty minutes later they were being greeted by their daughters, Jennie and Corinne with little Dominic.

11

Return to No-man's-land

THE GOOSSENS' arrival in London coincided almost exactly
with Armistice Day, but the year was 1962. The family had
rather naturally tended to regard Léon's homecoming as
the focal point of his recovery. Indeed, the surgeon had
done his handiwork so well that by this time, with a
generously brown complexion, Léon looked to all intents
and purposes, the picture of health.

Only he knew how incomplete the story was; no doctor,
specialist or dental surgeon, nor even his own devoted wife,
could hope to be aware of the devastating numbness and the
lack of control he felt when he placed the reed of his oboe in
his mouth. It would take a fellow musician fully to appreciate
his predicament.

Léon settled down in grim determination to try and evoke
some response from his lips, but with little marked success.
Two weeks later he was feeling much depressed and looked a
picture of hopeless dejection. His family would often walk
into the room to catch him looking vacantly into nowhere;
alternatively he would spend hours gazing at the television
set with little apparent interest. He would brighten up when
brought into conversation, but he seemed to have been
overtaken by a sudden disinterest in the world about him.

The situation was not improved by the impending court

case. Whereas his family practitioner was endeavouring with all his might to effect a cure, the specialists who were examining Léon, seemed to be probing with infinite pains to establish the extent of the permanent injury, and now the lawyers were adding their own weighty words. This was not the world of the sensitive musician. Suddenly, with counsel arraigned on either side, the oboe player found himself in the midst of a legal battle.

It was, in fact, to protect his interests that the mighty guns were being brought to bear. It appeared to all concerned more than possible that Léon might never effectively play again. His family were long lived, as the record shows, and he might reasonably look forward to another twenty-five years of comfortable life. Should his standard of living, indeed his very livelihood, be placed in jeopardy through the carelessness at least of another motorist? Indeed not, his wife and advisers would correctly opine. Counsel on both sides required him to be specially examined by their own medical consultants, with a view to establishing a yardstick for compensation. This is part of the report prepared by an eminent neuro-surgeon.

"I examined Mr. Goossens who told me that the thing which worried him most was that he spent all his time now wondering if he could keep a certain engagement. He said that he should be playing a concerto at the Wigmore Hall tonight, which would occupy thirteen to fifteen minutes of playing. Although he practises and tries, he feels that he has no muscles in his lower lip sufficient to press the lower lip up against the reed and sustain the embouchure. In playing the oboe certain changes of tone and the amount of sound are produced by relaxing the pressure on the variable aperture of the reed. If high notes are required—extreme top notes— high pressure must be sustained against the reed, and he finds that with his lip in its present condition, he cannot sustain this pressure. Therefore the note may break with a fall of pitch. In playing the oboe, the reed resistance varies with the temperature, therefore extreme sensitivity of the lip is necessary to make the fine adjustments in order to correct variable pitch arising from temperature change during the performance. Owing to the anaesthesia of his lip and impairment of muscle power, Mr. Goossens feels that he cannot be certain of giving an adequate performance.

"Describing the feeling in his lip, he said that he has a tingling, a lack of sensation in both sides of his lower lip, right across and in the centre. It feels as if the muscle has been destroyed and there is nothing there at all. Both sides of the lower lip are thickened by scar tissue. In fact, the feeling that there is no muscle is due to lack of sensation at this point, the actual muscular bulk being quite adequate.

"This physical disability has produced a secondary emotional disability. Goossens states that he would hate to retire, that he hates missing the concerts, that his disability has given him a terrible feeling of inferiority. He says he has very bad nights, he wakes at 2 or 3 or 4 in the morning and starts worrying and longing for breakfast time to come. He is terrified that he might not be able to play again."

The report is a long one and comments upon the intelligence tests which Léon was asked to perform. The results of these were excellent. It concludes with these sentences:

"Examination of the nervous system shows no evidence of any nystagmus or rombergism. Therefore such minor giddiness as he now experiences will also subside as time passes. The degree of recovery at this stage of time indicates that there will be no intellectual deficit resulting from his concussion."

Referring to a detailed physical examination of the lower part of the face, it says:

"Examination of the lower lip shows firstly that the mucosa in the midline where it joins the lower jaw comes on to the gum at an abnormally high level, either because it has been sutured at that level at operation, or because following the sloughing of the mucosa, it healed in an abnormal position. The effect of this abnormality is that it tends to fix the lip down and interfere with efforts to pull the lip over the lower teeth upwards to make an embouchure. I believe that there is no doubt that the function of the lip could be improved if this abnormality were corrected by a plastic operation. The lip is tied down, rather in the same way as the tongue is tied down in a patient born with a congenital abnormality of tongue tie. Apart from that, the bulk of muscle in the lower lip is very good, although this drags on the gum when he forces the lip out. There is also full upward pressure of the lip. The lip is somewhat thickened at both sides where suturing has been performed, but this itself would not interfere to any great extent with this gentleman's playing.

"Examination of the sensation in the lip is encouraging for there is full sensation in the mucosa and full sensation over the mucous membrane of the lip, but in the skin area, in the midline, there is an area of defective sensation measuring slightly over half an inch at the mucosa and tapering down to about a quarter of an inch wide, half an inch below the level of the mucosa. This area is not totally insensitive, but is the seat of paraethesia, and this suggests that the nerve fibres are growing into this area and *ultimately* sensation may be restored in the lip."

This professional opinion was dated January 2, 1963, and represents the situation just under six months after the operation. There were to be many further examinations and a particularly interesting one a year later. In the meantime, having assessed the physical condition, the lawyers decided they should step across the gulf that separates those plain words with a keen appraisal that should be sought from an eminent musician.

Consequently an approach was made to Sir Arthur Bliss, Master of the Queen's Musick. He had known Léon on and off for many years, indeed they had travelled to America together between the wars. Without doubt a conductor who was familiar with his previous performance was in a privileged position to judge the musical effect of the accident upon the career of the oboist.

He wrote, "In my view the ability to play the oboe depends on breath control and sensitivity, particularly of the lower lip. To a great player like Mr. Goossens, the embouchure is all-important, as important indeed as vocal chords to a singer. Mr. Goossens received injuries which affected his lips, and I am of the opinion that they cannot be patched up or repaired so as to enable him to produce the same continuity of phrasing as was possible prior to the accident. Mr. Goossens also lost many teeth in the accident and, again, I feel that this materially affected his powers of control and makes it virtually impossible for him to perform all the great works that have been written for and dedicated to him."

This passage made sombre reading, but by this time, Léon was tired of the legal rigmarole which seemed to him an almost unnecessary complication in the circumstances. His one desire in life was to play the oboe again, not to be concerned in cornering a careless motorist. He began to increase the tempo of his practice, judged not so much by the number of hours that he put in, for his lips were quite unable to manage more than a few sustained minutes of playing, but by stepping up the frequency of the sessions.

However, his daily bread had to be earned and Léon was determined that whatever the outcome of the legal battle, he must seek alternative employment, either as a part-time teacher or—horrible thought—as a full time member of the staff of a music college. Nevertheless there was a rub, for not only did he have to admit that he was somewhat over forty, but further that he had begun steadily to ascend the scale above sixty-five! At this age most teachers are contemplating their cottage in the country.

He even journeyed to Yorkshire for an interview, but fortunately for British music the gods frowned upon this base idea. He was offered the post but Léon decided that it was just too much to tear up his roots in London and transport himself to the Yorkshire Dales, or more accurately a slightly less lovely West Riding town. He returned chastened and all the more determined that somehow he would bring his reed to speak again.

12

Back to Work

IT WAS nearly two months before Léon Goossens was finally pronounced fit enough for discharge. In fact, he took his farewell of Epsom Hospital on December 27, 1918, after a riotous Christmas. The future stretched before him as a gaping void.

During the often tedious years of trench warfare, he had been thinking deeply. Not only had there been an abrupt and clean break with his previous existence, but he had also lived in the company of a fascinating mixture of men who hailed from all parts of the world.

One such boy, for most of them were still really boys although they had lived a capsuled lifetime of experience, had been manager on a South American ranch. He was in the 29th Fusiliers from the Legion of Frontiersmen, and the two became firm friends. "It's a tremendous life out there," he persuaded Léon, "why not come out and have a shot at it?"

On many occasions, as a corporal in the trenches, Léon had tried to picture in the mind his beloved instrument, but he had found that he could not recall even the fingering. Besides which he loved the open air life, and the time he had spent with the horses in Dublin had kindled a life-long interest in all matters equine.

In fact, one of his most stirring memories of the war was concerned with horses—two of them drawing an ambulance through "Death Valley". It was a depression in the sweeping terrain through which the Scarpe River flowed.

The horse-drawn vehicle, resembling an early covered wagon, with a giant red cross painted on each side; came into sight, on a return journey from the forward sector. They were already at full gallop, having obviously been observed, for an enemy gun with malevolent intent, was dropping shells in a line behind them.

The animals looked absolutely magnificent with flowing manes and tails, but it is doubtful, if occupants there were, whether they would have survived the journey! The horses had the bits between their teeth and the soldier driving them was barely in command, hanging on to the reins like grim death. It was a miracle that he was not thrown to the ground. On and on they thundered, crashing and lurching over the badly pitted surface of the road, until miraculously they disappeared from sight down the far side of the range of hills, presumably to safety, if they could be brought to a standstill!

*　　　*　　　*

Léon's young friend did not have too much difficulty in persuading him. They met in London for a meal shortly after Léon's discharge. The erstwhile oboist had become extremely unsettled. His eight weeks' inactivity had only tended to make matters that much worse.

"Are you still coming?" the question was put to him.

"Of course," the ex-musician earnestly replied.

"Jolly good show."

"Have to break it gently to my parents, of course. What will I need?"

"Well," said the rancher thoughtfully, "You can't enter the country without capital of £100 and then there's the fare . . ."

Léon's face clouded momentarily.

"Hmmm," he said. "I'll have to speak to Dad."

In due course, after a good evening spent in each other's company, Léon returned home. It so happened that his father walked in at the same moment, following his evening conducting.

"Hello, Lee," he said kindly.

"Hello, Dad."

For Papa Goossens it was strange to renew close contact with the spare young figure of a boy who had returned as a man. How grateful he was that his young son had been spared.

Léon knew it would be hard to tell his father, and his heart faltered, but he had to go on.

"Dad," he began hesitatingly. "There are one or two things that I have been thinking over . . ."

"Of course, Lee," his parent said understandingly. "Come on in."

And then he blurted out the story, half told with enthusiasm, half with a feeling of dread as to how his stern parent would react to the news.

The telling was made that much harder because as Léon looked at the face of his father, he could see a new onrush of years, not clearly marked for all to see, but visible to the penetrating gaze of a much loving youngest son. He felt he was telling of treachery, but he had underestimated his father, who was a man of wisdom.

"I quite understand, Lee," he said generously, "I quite understand."

He fell silent for some minutes, and gazed deeply into the last dust covered embers of the fire, but his mind was working keenly. This was a natural reaction, he appreciated. It hurt him to think of what his young son had been called upon to endure, but the thought of such talent as he possessed being allowed to fly out of the window was something he could not

G

bear to contemplate. If only he could rekindle that inborn love for music, the battle might yet be won. Then came his sagacious inspiration.

"Look, Lee," he said, smiling, "there's the question of the £100 and, of course, your fare. I would like to help you . . ." His voice and words held just the right amount of hesitancy and Léon was quick to respond.

"Good Lord, no, Dad. I don't want it from you. I can easily earn it," and brilliantly his father cut in. "Of course you can. I know, you must get out your oboe! I am sure after a week or so it will all come back. I can even arrange to get you some work. You will soon earn your £100 pounds."

This was not quite what Léon had had in mind, but certainly it seemed a reasonable suggestion. After all, what else could he do?

"Good idea. I'll go round and pick it up from the bank tomorrow."

He rose from his seat, stretching his limbs, as likewise did his father, he rested his hand lightly on his son's shoulder.

"We are very glad to have you home, Lee," and, as he said it, Léon could feel the very slightest tremor in his father's hand.

"By the way," he said as they walked from the room. "Let's not tell Mum for a day or two. It might upset her. We'll pick a suitable time."

"Of course," Léon replied, and stood back to allow his father to walk up the stairs. Indeed it was good to be home again.

The following day it was cold and wintry, with a cheerless sky and throwing on a top coat after his breakfast, Léon decided to walk down through the gardens and pick up a bus to Piccadilly. He would then pass his old college, for old times sake.

In that institution they were also having difficulties with returning ex-servicemen home from the war. There was Douglas Fox, whose first instrument had been the piano. He had come back, minus one arm, and he lived under a perpetual cloud of despondency. Nothing anyone did could evoke a response.

His professor was Dr. Hugh Allen.* Here was another wise man. He could not fail to notice the torment within his young student, and suddenly, much to everybody's surprise, Dr. Allen disappeared for a week, and nobody knew where or why. When he did come back he called Douglas Fox to the office.

"Come in and sit down, Fox," he said kindly. "You know I've been away for a week . . . just got back . . . I have been working on an experiment."

The face of the young man sitting before him wrinkled in perplexity.

"An experiment, sir?"

"Yes," said Dr. Allen. "I have lived the whole of last week with one of my arms strapped behind my back. I wanted to see for myself just how difficult life would be if I found myself in a similar position to you."

His voice was unemotional, matter of fact. "You know, Fox, I found there was simply nothing I could not do. I could even play the piano. Now I've tried, I think you should try too."

This little demonstration of interest and understanding had a remarkable effect. Douglas Fox turned over a new leaf, looked at life from a different angle, fighting back the frustration and overcoming his disability. He became, and still is, a brilliant organist. When Fox plays it would take a first class musician to detect that the organist has but one arm, and to watch him at his instrument is an incredible sight. His hand seems to move at the speed of light, travelling over the keys, manipulating the stops, all, it appears, in a single movement, and out flows the music, beautifully controlled without perceptible hesitation.

As Léon passed the Round Pond, it was to find that no one was playing with their boats, the day being cold.

* Later Sir Hugh Allen.

Indeed, there was a thin, smooth layer of ice upon the water, with an occasional break kept open by the movement of the wildfowl. He was shortly sitting on a bus, resavouring the experience with relish.

By the time he reached Piccadilly, Léon was chilled and stiff. Alighting, he walked briskly down Pall Mall and shortly after ten, entered the bank. He handed them a slip of paper and waited interminably while the clerk disappeared into the vaults. Eventually he returned, dusting as he did so, the black case of Léon's oboe.

"Many thanks," said Léon, his heart warming at the sight of his instrument, and clutching it in his hand, he walked briskly back to the bus stop. He had a strong desire to open the case on his lap, but he resisted it until, finally, he reached Edith Road.

He slipped quietly into the music room, and extracted the oboe with care. It looked exactly as he had left it three years before. He flicked it with his handkerchief and assembled it with a tingling sense of excitement.

Glancing quickly at the door to see that it was closed, he raised the reed to his lips. Suddenly he found himself running up a scale and down again. He almost surprised himself that he had done it; so he did it again. The tone was beautiful and clear, and as the sound filled the room, he felt his spirits lifting.

More than anything else he was amazed at his fingers, the self-same fingers that had become so hard and cruel caressing a Lee Enfield rifle, now reverting, softly and tenderly, to a full range of flexibility.

In something approaching a fever of excitement, he looked round for a piece of music. Suddenly his mother at the other end of the house heard the wondrous sound, and stopping a moment to listen to it, she could not resist the temptation to go in and see her youngest son returning to his music. He heard her open the door, but did not look up nor did he stop playing. She stood there smiling for a moment or two, then turned and left the room. Her heart was singing. Yes, thought Léon, I'll soon be able to earn £100!

* * *

Father Goossens was more nervous than he let on. Léon had now announced his intention to the family, and it was going to be a damned close run thing.

In 1919 the task of finding work for a gifted young oboist proved not to be a difficult one. Engagements followed rapidly one upon another, and gradually the balance in his bank began to mount, but as his wise parent had prayed, so also was his interest being surely rekindled.

It was a few weeks after his return to the world of the professional musician that Léon's young friend contacted him again.

"How are you doing, Léon? Have you raised the £100 yet?"

"Yes, I have managed that," the young oboist somewhat diffidently replied.

"Thank heavens for that. I'm leaving for South America in ten days' time."

"Oh," Léon murmured. His pal could easily detect the hesitancy in his friend's voice.

"What's the problem then?" he enquired.

"Well, it's my engagements . . ." Léon tried to explain. "I seem to have got so many of them. Certainly I don't see how I could manage to come for a few weeks yet."

As Papa Goossens had astutely gambled, this difficulty was never resolved!

* * *

Léon Goossens rejoined the Queen's Hall Orchestra as principal oboist. On the morning that he attended his first rehearsal, which coincided with the commencement of a new season, he sat down at his place, having given the orchestra an "A", when Sir Henry Wood duly arrived, and traditionally shook hands with all the principals. Coming upon young

Léon, after the interval of some three bloody years, he remarked, "Good morning, Mr. Goossens, glad to see you back. Had a nice time?"

*   *   *

It was in the year following Léon's return from Malta that he found he could just manage to attain such a standard as would allow him to try his hand and his nerve by playing in the film music recording sessions. There is no doubt whatsoever that the therapeutic effect of rejoining his friends and colleagues in the little orchestra did much to bolster his confidence, although the physical limitations were severe.

He also began giving lectures with records to music clubs and gramophone societies which was the nearest he could get to personal performance. A local Hertfordshire newspaper reported at the time:

"He illustrated his highly entertaining lecture by playing short pieces on the oboe, but explained to his audience, 'I find it difficult to sustain long pieces, as yet'."

The last two words are worth noting, for as difficult as the problems were that faced Léon Goossens, his whole mental approach was one of determination to struggle back to his former virtuoso playing.

It was at about this time that an American came into contact with the film music orchestra. He was comparatively unknown as a conductor and obtained his income from recording film music. It was often more convenient, and invariably cheaper, to arrange these sessions in London. It was not long before Gene Forrell became friendly with Léon and familiar with the predicament of the oboist. He was to have a profound effect upon him.

The year 1963 in the Goossens calendar was a black one. The frustration of his physical disability and the constant fear that perhaps after all there would never be a comeback made the months both long and despairing. Their daughter,

Jennie, married, and Léon decided to sell his house and move to a smaller one.

He realised now that he would have to face a long hard struggle. He came to the decision to try and evolve a new technique in his playing. To do so he would have to bring into use muscles not usually required in playing the oboe. It was difficult in the extreme, and this is best illustrated by a medical report of a second examination by the specialist who had seen him previously. It was now something just under two years since the accident.

"On my last tests on March 9, 1964, there was a distinctly diminished sensitivity lying in this area, and his ability to hold between his lips and keep horizontal, a lightweight object—comparable to a cigarette holder—was much less than could be expected. Repeat tests showed that the lower lip tired quickly.

"The conclusion I reached was that both the sensory and motor functions of the nerve branches in the lower lip from both right and left inferior maxillary nerves are much impaired some twenty months after the accident. They are unlikely to improve in the future to any marked extent."

At this juncture Lord Brain's advice was also sought and he generally concurred with the specialist's opinion.

Hence the need for a new technique, but there was another dark cloud looming over the head of Léon Goossens. He is a modest and shy man by nature, and each day brought the prospect of a legal battle in the law courts that much nearer.

Eminent counsel had been concluding their briefs and although Léon was told that he had simply nothing to worry about, he was nevertheless filled with dread of the occasion. In fact it was his compassion for the man on the other side which caused him his deep concern.

Suddenly and miraculously, the clouds were swept aside. After further examinations by the opposing side's medical experts, the defendants asked for terms to settle out of court!

It was shortly after this great burden had been lifted from

Léon's mind that Gene Forrell, who had become a good friend, put forward a suggestion.

"Léon, why not work towards a comeback and stage it in America?"

This suggestion was a staggering one, but the reasoning was as follows.

Forrell, a proficient musician, had had to support himself in the world of commercialism. However, he now wished to enter a more serious field. Léon, on the other hand, enjoyed a world wide reputation, but had been forced to endure two years of concert inactivity, although each month his new technique was beginning to show signs of improvement and his ability to sustain longer periods of playing was gradually giving him cause for qualified optimism.

Being an enthusiast, Forrell positively swept aside all the barriers of negation thrown up by Léon Goossens.

"We'll give a baroque concert in the town hall of New York! It will be marvellous for both of us. The great Léon Goossens to play again and I shall have the honour of conducting. What do you say, Léon?"

The oboist was taken completely by surprise.

"It's a splendid idea, Gene, but . . . but it would take at least another year . . ."

"Who cares! It's something to aim for. I'm prepared to wait, if you're prepared to try?"

Ever since Eugène had arranged Léon's first tour in America, he had reserved an affectionate place in his heart for that country and its people.

"I'll try," he declared slowly and solemnly. But it has to be reported that the timbre of his voice did not betray of over-much enthusiasm.

Slowly the wheels were beginning to turn again. Life once more would have some direction. Even more than Léon, his wife jumped at the idea.

"You must, darling, you simply must," Leslie declared.

RIGHT : Leslie and mischievous grandson Dominic Spence.

BELOW : Two brothers at the height of their careers, Léon and Eugène.

LEFT : Sir Eugène Goossens, conductor.

BELOW : Portrait of a happy family.

13

The New World

In 1924, following family tradition, Léon entered upon the world of opera by joining the Covent Garden Orchestra as principal oboist. They began with a production of the Wagner "Ring" commencing with *Rhinegold*. Lotte Lehmann, Elizabeth Schumann and Frederick Shorr were the principals.

The music of these operas was marvellous to play and it was an exhilarating experience to perform under the baton of Bruno Walter, Kleiber, Rheiner and Krauss, among many others.

Then came the season of ballet, commencing with *Swan Lake* followed by *Petrouchka* danced by George Balanchine. Then there was Massine in *The Three Cornered Hat*, and Léon watched, when he was able, Karsavina, Lydia Sokolova and Serge Lifar.

The Goossens reputation was growing, so much so that a leading oboist in one of the foremost Italian opera houses having heard him play declared, "I am willing to break my instrument over my knee after listening to such perfection."

From a fellow musician, this was praise indeed, but perhaps the greatest accolade of his entire career was the moment after a Prom. at the Albert Hall when his father went back-stage following the first performance in England of the Strauss Oboe Concerto and said, "You are a great artist, Lee, a great artist." These few words from his sternest critic had taken thirty years to achieve, and they made Léon's heart warm. Nothing anyone wrote or said before or since ever gave him a feeling of greater joy. He had succeeded.

Within the Goossens family, it could be said that if favourite there was, it was Eugène who basked in perpetual sunshine, especially in the eyes of his mother. Zen and Lee's voices coincided in timbre. One day Léon telephoned home and his mother answered the call.

"Hello, Mum," he began, to which she responded, "Oh, hello, darling . . .", but realising from the tone of her voice that she had made a mistake in identity, he said quietly, "It's Lee." "Oh," she replied quickly. "It's you, is it."

But Zen was a wonderful elder brother and Léon treated his slightly favoured position with no more than a laugh or a wry smile. In fact, it was Eugène, now working in America, who counselled him that he must make his début in that fine country, "but you will need a special new work to play. I know, I'll write something for you."

This was probably one of Eugène Goossen's finest compositions, a concerto for oboe and orchestra. When Léon set sail, the work had not been completed, and finally Eugène was only to manage a pianoforte arrangement.

He sailed on the Cunarder *Alaunia*, calling at Halifax, Nova Scotia, where Léon saw and met his theatrical idols, Seymour Hicks and Ellaline Terriss.

In New York he stayed at the Majestic Hotel, as guest of Eugène. The concert took place at the Guild Theatre and the composition and performance took one music critic, at least, by surprise.

"Have you ever heard a concerto for oboe? Such a thing assuredly is a novelty, like Andres Segovia, who achieves amazing results with the guitar. Léon Goossens (brother of

the distinguished English conductor, Eugène Goossens)
makes his chosen instrument stand forth conspicuously; and
his début in this country a few afternoons ago was a note-
worthy occasion. I do not recall any programme having been
given in this country in which the oboe has been featured.

"Assisted by brother Eugène at the piano, and The
Marianne Kneisel String Quartet, Léon Goossens demon-
strated his right to a place among the elect."

The *Telegraph* also covered the event.

"The novelty of the weekend, if not the week, was the oboe
recital of Léon Goossens, brother of the composer.

"The sweet-throated pastoral instrument was its plaintive
and whimsical self in a variety of colour patterns, kaleido-
scopic and amazing. We think of the oboe among instruments as the 'Lass with the Delicate Air'. She did not step
out of her character, to be sure—she could not be other than
herself—yet there was a scope of performance, in the hands,
or at the lips, of Léon Goossens which presented a new vista
of tonal possibilities. One noted the absence of reed licking,
so common with most players of the oboe. And in the difficult passages of his programme, the artist recalled Heifetz.

"One is tempted to say of Léon Goossens that he is the
greatest player of the oboe."

Following this acclaim, new engagements were speedily
forthcoming. Léon journeyed to Rochester and marked the
occasion with his first serious brush with a motor car.

The weather was bitterly cold; indeed the street outside
the Sagamore Hotel was transformed to a sheet of ice. Being
careful as guest in a foreign country to observe the rules of
the road, Léon stood patiently at the traffic signals, waiting
for them to turn in his favour, then proceeded to walk across
the icy street.

Suddenly he noticed the car some fifty yards away,
endeavouring to stop; but it was immediately apparent that
the driver was unable to do so. Even as Léon tried vainly to

LORD CHAMBERLAIN'S OFFICE,

ST JAMES'S PALACE, S.W.1.

21st Jan 1931

WORCESTER. P.T.O

Dear Léon:

Alas! I have been a martyr t[o] sciatica ever since I had the pleasure of seeing you: I have managed to keep over two engagements but [illegible] on. However I have [illegible]
th

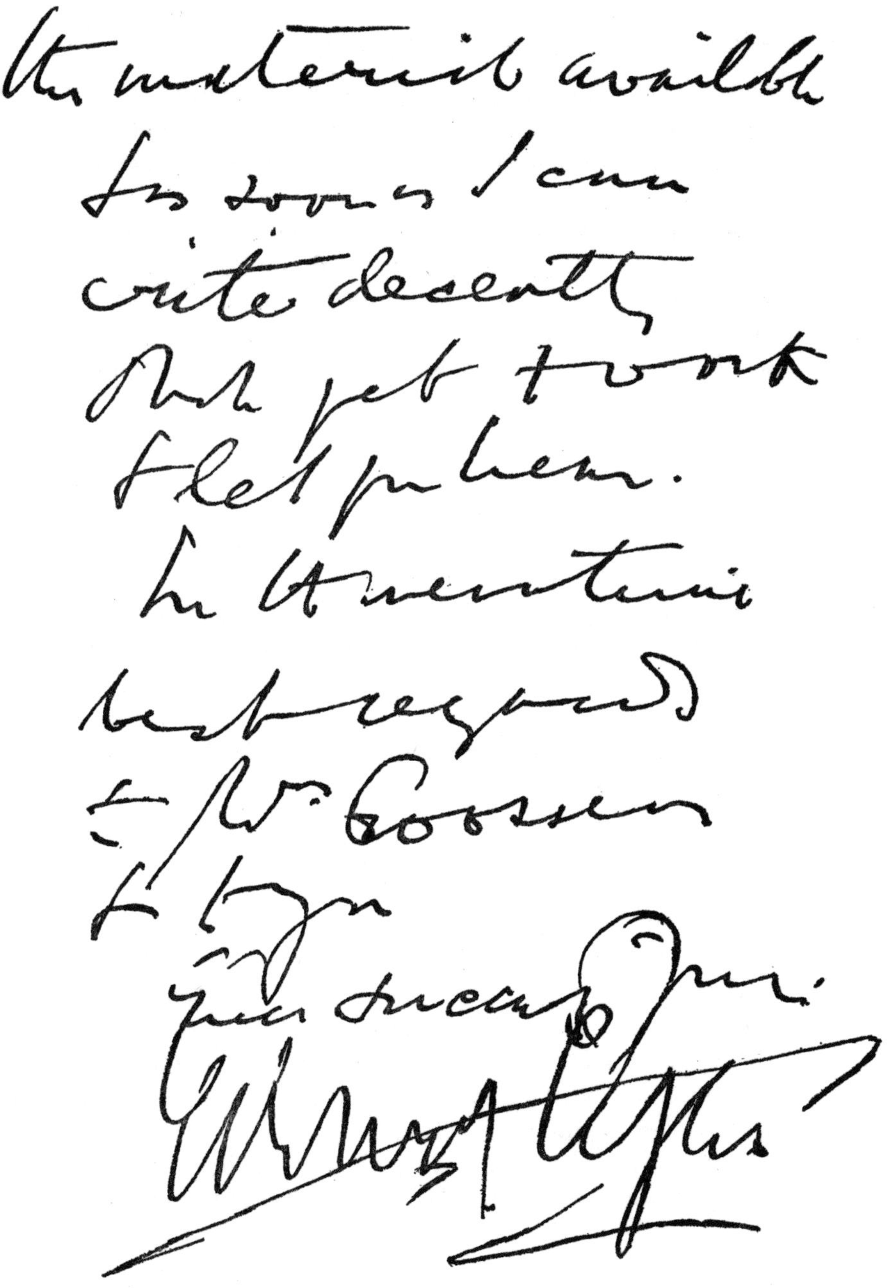
the materials available
as soon as I can
write decently
such jobs to work
& let you hear.
[illegible]

best regards
to Mr. Goossens
& to you
Yours sincerely
Edward Elgar

Facsimile of Elgar's letter referred to on page 102.

move out of the way, he knew that it was impossible, for he could hardly keep upon his feet. Almost at the moment of impact, in a sudden inspiration, he leapt towards the car, pitching his hand carrying his oboe case towards the windscreen. Thus spreadeagled across the bonnet, he just managed to avert being dragged underneath, until gradually the momentum of the car fell away, as Léon himself toppled off. He escaped with only a few minor scratches and bruises, and was pleased to continue on his way, somewhat shaken, to take part in his concert but one hour later.

Upon his return to England, Léon, who was by now professor of the oboe at both the Royal College of Music and the Royal Academy, found that engagements were pouring in. He began to travel the world and to meet many renowned composers and musicians. First Berlin then Florence, until gradually he became familiar with all the great capitals.

He was friendly with Elgar, indeed taught him the rudiments of driving a motor car, and that great English composer, shortly before his death, was engaged upon writing a new oboe suite, upon the fly-leaf of which he had penned Léon's name. Unfortunately only the slow movement was completed, but Léon treasures the manuscript to this day although he was to wait until his seventieth birthday in 1967 to perform it for the first time. Elgar explained in a letter penned on January 21st, 1931, how his sciatica made it virtually impossible to write. (See pages 100 and 101.)

He found himself playing with the world's greatest instrumentalists, and it was Fritz Kreisler who said, "If there's one thing more than another I enjoy playing in the whole violin literature, it's the Andante from the Brahms Concerto with Léon Goossens playing the oboe."

But, in spite of all this, the oboist firmly believed that he had a long way to go, and he struggled to further his technique, always striving after an unassailable perfection. Composers began to regard the instrument with fresh favour, and

Léon frequently found himself called upon to introduce new works supported so often by the flawless accompaniment of such wonderful artists as Gerald Moore and Ivor Newton.

The following letter from Rutland Boughton, penned on February 18, 1938, is interesting, not only because it sets down the opinion of the composer of Léon Goossens' playing, but also as a reminder that it is difficult indeed to satisfy any composer absolutely!

My dear Leon,

    I must just send you a word of deep thanks for your beautiful performance yesterday—I especially marvelled at the instinctive rightness of the nuances in the first and third movements. That is the soul of artistry that only comes by the gift of the gods, plus human industry—I believe that another time you might find the slow movement more satisfactory if the beginning and end were less emotional—I have always felt it as a very calm restrained thing, except for a little self-revelation in the middle, where you were absolutely right. Now I want to hear you do Number 2.

Yours very gratefully,
Rutland B.

Both Léon and his brother Eugène took particular delight in bringing the work of new composers before the public. Such a man was Boughton, born in Aylesbury on January 23, 1878. His father had been a small grocer and his son's musical education was as different from Léon's as could possibly be imagined. He was in his early teens when he finally decided to become a composer. However, it was only through the interest and enthusiasm of Sir Charles Stanford that he was able to study at the Royal College of Music. As Michael Hurd noted, "The opportunities for the performance of any English opera at this time, and for many years to come, were negligible. For a man who is determined to create a new style, and had declared himself in sympathy with beliefs that many people held to be dangerous, the prospects were overwhelmingly unfavourable."

He was to write to Léon again some thirteen years before his death.

My dear Leon,

Joy tells me that it was a lovely performance, and the broadcast (which we can't get here) even better. I thank you with all my heart. While we have artists of your calibre, the world is not such a bad place. You would make any work sound good.

Yours ever,
Rutland.

Léon had the pleasure of playing Boughton's Concerto Number One for Oboe and Strings at Salzburg on the occasion of the visit of the Boyd Neel Orchestra.

*   *   *

Vaughan Williams wrote a new concerto and this time it was through a suggestion by the B.B.C. that oboist and composer were brought together. For this performance alterations were being made up to the final hour. Vaughan Williams wrote:

Dear Goossens,

I hear from the B.B.C. that they have asked you to play my new concerto at the Proms. I need hardly say I am much pleased at the prospect, if you are also pleased—but you had better see it before you make up your mind! I hope to send you the oboe part and a pianoforte reduction of the score in about a fortnight. Of course, I shall welcome any suggestions from you as to making the part more "oboistic". The accompaniment is scored for strings only. There are three movements, 1 the Rondopastoral, 2 Minuet & Musetta, 3 Finale (Scherzo). The whole work plays well under twenty minutes.

Yours sincerely,

Fourteen days later he wrote:

Herewith the score of the concerto. Don't blame Mullinar for its untidy state—I altered it all after he had made it!

Yours etc.,

Vaughan Williams.

In 1937, Léon Goossens was invited to perform the Bach Concerto with the London Philharmonic Orchestra under the baton of Sir Thomas Beecham, for whom he had worked for many years. Some weeks preceding the concert, there was some interesting correspondence with Sir Donald Tovey, who wrote to Léon from Edinburgh.

8th November, 1937.

Dear Goossens,

Here is all the material I can collect without undue delay. Besides this you will need a sufficiency of all string parts in the Breitkopf and Haertell edition of the Clavier Concertos. What I send is the *absolutely essential* continuo part, as filled out by me. It can be played on the harpsichord to satisfy the consciences of the high-brows, and to disappoint Philipp Emanuel and probably Bach himself. I thoroughly agree both with Philipp Emanuel and with Schweitzer that Bach put up with the harpsichord as an unpunctual nuisance, that does not blend with the strings and that half-way down the hall conveys only a faint impression of chewing the cud. The pianoforte, on the other hand, needs a very soft touch. You may remember that, when we did the C Minor Double Concerto, I had to oust a first-rate student from the pianoforte

H

and take the continuo myself, because his touch was too hard.

The other essential part of the continuo is a special desk of 'cellos, which in this concerto must supply such basis as Bach has transferred from the lost original to the clavier. To save time I have left blank all the bars that are the same as the extant 'cello part, so a good copyist must fill these in, either from a printed part or from the score. I am sorry that the continuo is not in a better handwriting than mine. Perhaps you may have the time to get a fresh copy made; or perhaps Sir Thomas may prefer something quite different. One of my principles is to avoid including ornamentation, which Bach had only because he was re-writing for the harpsichord. I regard as entirely un-Bachish to return detail that is unnecessary in the circumstances. Where the clavier is providing the only bass to the harmony, I must restore it to the violoncellos, as well as retaining it in the continuo; though, of course, where the strings really have complete harmony by themselves, I share Bach's pleasure in the fact.

You may remember that I restored your own part largely on the basis of information furnished by the preface and the appendix of Vol. XVII of the Bach-Gesellschaft. I can't be sure that I have done this consistently; and, of course, nobody can quarrel with you for adopting whatever you think fit of the clavier ornamentation. But I am myself convinced that most of it is a concession to the prickliness of the harpsichord, and that it would not only dehumanise and delocalise your instrument, but would blur some important outlines of form. I went into this thoroughly with the slow movement and finale, but I have a vague suspicion that I wasn't quite consistent in the first movement in the following bars: viz., 42, 82 and 84, in all of which I would read

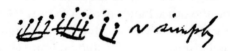

By the way, I see that Peter's have published an edition of the Concerto for Oboe and Violin, and that the editor has decided that it is in D minor. I am certain that he is wrong, not only because this would bring the oboe up to E, whereas Bach never writes above D, but because, if the original had not been in C Minor, there would have been no conceivable

reason why this

should become this

when the violin has to play it in a lower key.*

We should be very glad to hear your Handel Concerto, of which I myself defrauded my audience last year, but this oboe d'amore thing is so heavenly, that if it is not too tiring to play in the same evening with your brother's Concerto, we would welcome the rare opportunity of hearing it again. The score which I sent was, as you see, originally a hireling, which I have insisted on buying. It shews traces that the parts have been edited by someone who puts lights and shades into the tuttis, which I should consider rather dangerous. Modern editors don't seem to realise that 90 per cent of musical colour is the position of the chords, and that of the remainder, 8 per cent is the balance of tone, and the final 2 per cent the actual tone of the different instruments. This does not apply to the solo player, who is ex-officio a singer. I am just getting up to the third act of *Parsifal* with some excellent local singers who are surprised to find that

* The musical examples have been reproduced from Sir Donald Tovey's original letter.

the meticulous Wagner, with all his wonderful orchestra markings, gives no marks whatsoever to the solo voices, except one "piano" (to prevent a single top note being misunderstood as a climax). How few modern composers there are who have the sense to let you singers live on your breath. Believe me.

Yours sincerely,
Donald Tovey.

But in 1963 Léon Goossens was no longer able to play concertos and the prospect of his comeback in America thoroughly alarmed the oboist.

He had last visited New York a few months before the declaration of war in 1939. The occasion being the sponsorship by the British Council of two concerts on June 9 and 10 at which Sir Adrian Boult conducted the New York Philharmonic Orchestra at the World's Fair concert in Carnegie Hall.

The soloists were Léon Goossens and Solomon. Three entirely new works were written for the concert, one being Arnold Bax's Fifth Symphony and a Piano Concerto by Arthur Bliss, and, lastly, Vaughan Williams "Five Variants on Dives and Lazarus". Léon was to play, once again, the oboe concerto written by Eugène for his first recital in New York in 1927.

The public's reaction to the concerts was not far short of ecstatic, but in regard to the playing of Léon Goossens, perhaps the mood can best be caught in two letters written by friends to Eugène Goossens, who unfortunately was unable to be present. The first was dated June 9, 1939.

Dear Maestro,

You certainly should feel mighty proud of your little brother. He gave a tremendous performance at Carnegie Hall under Sir Adrian Boult, and I am rushing this letter off to make the morning sailing. I am not certain whether he received nine or eleven curtain calls after he had finished. Carnegie was quite packed, even in the $2·50 section, and the night was beastly torrid, I can assure you. But backstage his popularity was more than demonstrated, he drew all the females from 12 to 100 years of age and seemed to have a job getting rid of them! So you can see, he's getting on all right! But seriously he did make a huge hit, and New York as "cold" as she is, liked him tremendously.

The second letter is dated the following day, and was signed by A. Walter Kramer.

Dear Gene, (as he was known in the States)

Just a few lines in my enthusiasm, to tell you that I heard your brother Léon yesterday at the first of the two British concerts, and that I must tell you that I have NEVER heard anything like him!

I introduced myself to him at the luncheon we gave Sir Adrian at the Beethoven Association yesterday, at which your brother and Bliss were also guests of honour. Naturally I referred to you and we had a pleasant chat for a few moments. In the evening I went to the concert, heard him, and shouted "Bravo!" with the rest of the big audience (Carnegie Hall). I went back to the artist's room after and congratulated him. He is *phenomenal*. I have just never heard anything like him. I told him that I did not know that what he does could be done on the oboe! and I mean just that.

Your concerto pleased me *greatly*. Don't think if I have referred first to your brother's playing that I wasn't listening to your music, which work was new to me. It is a beautiful piece, both in conception and execution, and the orchestra did its part finely.

Pardon this brief note. I want it to go to you without delay

to tell you how great a success your brother had with your
music.

With every good wish,

Yours, etc.

Now Léon Goossens found himself being swept along
towards a new and even more exacting début in the United
States of America. In order to give him yet greater time to
prepare, it was decided that the concert should take place in
the spring of 1965. This would mean that there had been an
enforced interlude of just over two and a half years since the
time of his accident. Léon enjoyed his sixty-eighth birthday
in June and began to practise even harder.

14

Come-back

ON THE day after it was announced in the press that Léon Goossens had been awarded a C.B.E. in the New Year's Honours List of 1950, he received a letter from his ageing father, who was now enjoying the autumn of his years in Finchley, north London.

2nd January, 1950.

Darling Lee,

I would be among the first of your innumerable admirers to congratulate you and applaud you on your nomination as confirmed in today's New Year's Honours List, at last enhanced by the mention of your name, nobly upheld in your service to art and by excellence of your own! What can I say more except that I wish you ever increasing renown, happiness and prosperity.

Always,
Dad.

With fondest love to you all.

It was fitting that in 1937 Papa Goossens should himself have been honoured by his own country, which was reported in London's *Evening News*, the final paragraph of which read: "His brilliant children are the best reason why Papa

576. High R:
4: Finchley.
London N.2
2: Jan'y/50.

Darling Len!

 I would be among the first of your innumerable admirers to congratulat-
and applaud you on your nomination. a
Conspicus in to days "New Years Honours List:
this last enhanced by the inclusion of your
name ..nobly upheld in your Services to Art..
and by excellence of your own!
 What can I say more. except that I
wish you ever increasing Renown Happiness
and Prosperity .

    Always
     Dad

With fondest Love
 to you all!

Facsimile of letter from Papa Goossens referred to on page 111.

Early professional engagement; South Pier Blackpool 1911. The youthful Oboe player determined to be seen (fifth from right back row). Adolphe, (horn) extreme left back row.

LEFT: Back from the war and about to embark on a brilliant career. RIGHT: 'In action' Second World War. Entertaining and entertained by the Royal Navy, Scapa Flow 1942.

ABOVE : Léon Goossens and Yehudi Menuhin listen to the playback at the recording just prior to the accident.

LEFT : Earnest discussion with conductor Colin Davis.

Goossens, small and gentle-voiced, with a full beard parted in the centre, should be decorated by his country. He has lived in England since he was seven, but has remained a Belgian."

He was, in fact, made a Chevalier of the Order of the Crown of Belgium.

*   *   *

During the latter months of 1964, Gene Forrell was constantly chivvying and encouraging Léon towards the preparation of his concert. The American for his part, being as good as his word, booked the Town Hall in New York and contracted some of the finest musicians in the city, who played together under the title of the Master Virtuosi.

Considerable discussion took place as to which works Léon should perform. Whereas he was quietly confident, it would have been suicide to tax the muscles of his lips too greatly, yet he was determined to demonstrate, not only to the audience, but to his family and friends, that those works that he had selected would demand of all his old strength, mastery and skill.

He decided on the Concerto in G Major, from five keyboard sonatas of Scarlatti, and the Albinoni B Flat Concerto. This might be considered daring in the circumstances, but if this was to prove a comeback, it would require a colourful choice of music that afforded the best opportunity for the oboist.

Suddenly another catastrophe befell the family. Leslie, who had borne the brunt of the anxiety and strain for the past two years, contracted a serious heart condition and was immediately admitted to Brompton Hospital.

Léon was beside himself with concern, but fortunately no irreparable harm had been done. Two weeks later, under strict dietary and worry-free strictures, Leslie was allowed home, whereupon it became Léon's turn to escort his wife to Malta!

Upon their return Léon went about life in his usual well-ordered manner, giving his lectures and concerts whenever invited. But long and sustained playing he did not tackle.

He had decided to let matters take their course. He even forbore to over-practise, allowing nature to take its course, and being careful not to overtax his strength.

Leslie made a remarkable recovery and endeavoured to treat the coming recital as no more than a normal occurrence. However, both husband and wife were nervous, for each realised the stakes for which Léon was playing. It was to justify and prove that he might legitimately return to the concert platform. He could be satisfied with no less than complete acceptance, and quietly his heart began to fill with joy as he realised that at long last he was really making steady improvement. The task before him was a mountain to climb and he was already three parts of the way to the summit.

*   *   *

Suddenly, with breath-taking speed, it was spring. The daffodils were blooming in the park and America beckoned for the third occasion.

It was inevitable that the tension would increase. Léon was nervous for Leslie, because she had been warned not to fly too soon after her illness. Leslie was nervous for Léon for perfectly obvious reasons, but there was no turning back, and they began to prepare for their journey. Came the day when Léon at last had to strip down his beloved oboe, and settle it in its case cushioned on the purple velvet.

Twice he had been parted from his instrument since boyhood. The first time during World War I, but the second had been an odd experience in the extreme.

It was in the '20s, and after he had been playing at a concert in Brighton. Placing the case in the rear of the car, he had made towards London but realised that his fuel gauge was flicking dangerously low; he stopped the car and crossed to a garage to see if it was open. When he returned an odd feeling of disquiet made him turn round and glance behind. During the two or three moments he had been away his dispatch case containing his oboe had been stolen.

Léon was moved by such anger that he had seldom experienced outside the trenches of warfare. Who on earth would wish to steal his oboe? He immediately informed the police and offered a reward. He advertised, he passed the word round, but all to no avail. Only the dispatch case was washed up by the sea. He was left with no alternative but to order a new instrument.

One day, two years later, the telephone rang and an unknown voice asked to speak to Mr. Léon Goossens. The oboist replied that it was he.

"Would you be interested in seeing your oboe again?"

Léon simply could not believe his ears. How on earth could it have been identified? Who was this man speaking on the other end of the telephone line?

"Of course," Léon answered with mounting excitement.

"Very well," the stranger's voice replied. "Ring this number. You will find it in a little secondhand junk shop in south-east London. Incidentally," the caller continued, "it is described as a clarinet. You might find that it is your oboe."

With that the mysterious caller replaced his receiver. The whole thing seemed quite incredible. Who on earth would know his instrument? How could it have been identified? Almost unbelieving, Léon rang the number he had been given. A man's voice answered.

"Good morning. I understand that you are offering a clarinet for sale."

"Yes, sir, that's right," the shop-keeper replied.

"My name is Léon Goossens. I am looking for a clarinet. If I were to send my secretary round to collect it, would you be prepared to allow me to see it on approval?"

"Why, certainly, sir," came the reply.

"Very well. I'll send him round right away."

This matter was altogether too intriguing, and Léon in a fever pitch of excitement sent a friend upon his urgent mission. Léon Goossens was sceptical in the extreme and yet somehow the incident had a certain ring of truth, indeed it was too incredible to be otherwise. In an hour and a half his friend had returned. One glance was sufficient. There was his long lost oboe and, taking it out of its case, he pointed to his initials scratched upon the joints under the keys by a little boy twenty-five years before. Léon lifted the telephone and re-dialled the number.

"This is Léon Goossens speaking. Thank you for allowing me to see your instrument. Perhaps I should first point out to you that it is not a clarinet but an oboe, and it happens to belong to me! However, I am not anxious to ask any questions. I am much obliged. Good day to you."

In consequence of this experience so many years before, Léon Goossens never allows his oboe to stray far from his side. When he and Leslie boarded the aircraft at the beginning of the third week in April 1965, his oboe was part of his hand luggage!

*　　　　*　　　　*

For the third time in his life, Léon Goossens gazed in awe upon the concrete edifices of that magnificent city, New York, and he was greeted with all the old warmth the heart could desire.

Somehow, he could not help thinking of his brother Zen. America had been good to the Goossens family since the days of Aynsley Cook on tour prior to the Civil War. In a way it was a homecoming, but yet of necessity it would prove to be a field of battle, for all the world knows, no critics can be more devastating than those of the little old City of New York.

But there was no stopping now and, as if time were suddenly being accelerated, the dawn of April 25 swept over the city. For all those concerned it was a moment of emotions in turmoil not least for Léon Goossens. Let us leave it to the cool phrases of the *New York Times* on Monday, April 26, to paint the scene:

"Léon Goossens, oboist, appears with Master Virtuosi Ensemble. Baroque oboe concertos are not distinguished for their profundity but, in the hands of a master stylist, they can generate enough musical pleasure of an equally valid variety to refresh the mind's ear long after an ordinary evening of Bach or Bruckner has been forgotten.

"Such was the effect of Léon Goossens' playing with the Master Virtuosi of New York in the Town Hall last night, with Gene Forrell, the Ensemble's musical director, conducting. It seems incredible that the event should mark only the third professional visit to this city by so distinguished a musician as Mr. Goossens, and his first appearance here since the 1939 World Fair.

"Seeing him stride on stage, like an erect, well exercised Board Chairman of fifty-five or so, it seems incredible, too, that Mr. Goossens has been playing the oboe for more than fifty years. But the record shows that he will be sixty-nine in June, and that he has been playing since 1913.

"For nearly all that time, Mr. Goossens has held a position unusual in the world of wind players. He has been venerated as the Heifetz, Rubinstein and Casals of the oboe. Such a reputation, in this country, based entirely on recordings, is a formidable one to live up to, but Mr. Goossens showed effortlessly that he had not done it with mirrors (or the electronic equivalent), and his marvellous tone and impeccable technique are as freshly preserved as his unerring sense of style.

"Before he played a note, it was obvious that he was a man who had come to enjoy himself and, in the charming Concerto in G Major, arranged for him by Gordon Bryan, from five keyboard sonatas of Domenico Scarlatti, the objective and its fulfilment were shared with his splendid colleagues and by their fortunate listeners. In the Albinoni B Flat Concerto (Op. 7, No. 3, played in the edition of Bernhard Paumgartner) the oboist was no less admirable for his imaginative spirit than for the qualities already mentioned. The instrument was not merely played—it fairly sang. Trills and ornaments were executed with such an air of spontaneity that they served only to embellish the pleasure of the music, not to call attention to the difficulties that, for Mr. Goossens, apparently never existed.

"In addition to the purely musical satisfaction offered by the two concertos, there was an uncommon rapport between the soloist and the orchestra, and it communicated itself to the audience. Mr. Goossens seemed genuinely glad that he had given pleasure and this added a wholly appropriate element of humanity and warmth to the evening."

*   *   *

No mention of any accidents, it will be observed. No false sympathy required. Léon Goossens, professional musician, had returned.

There was but one more hurdle to conquer. Upon his return to England he was anxious to let it be known within the world of music, whose members might have been forgiven for writing off an oboist of such advancing years, that he was as good as ever. On May 16, 1966, the *Daily Telegraph* saw to it that justice might be done and that a file containing an accident report from Willesden General Hospital could finally be shut and locked away.

*   *   *

"LÉON GOOSSENS AT HIS BEST. It was well known that a few years ago, Léon Goossens, the supreme oboe player, severely damaged his mouth in a motoring accident. Although he lost all feeling in his lower lip, he would not accept defeat and began practising again in an attempt to recover his old mastery.

His recital at Macclesfield yesterday afternoon convinced the audience that his perseverance had been richly rewarded. The tone seemed as seductive, the control as effortless, the phrasing as immaculate, as ever.

The astonishing crescendos in Bach's Adagio seemed to materialise out of space at no given point in time, and grow and grow until they filled the hall. The last note of his encore, high and perfectly controlled, lingers in the memory."

*   *   *

There are no more Goossens in the male line but the blood, if not the name, has been passed into many daughters. It is to be hoped that the spirit as well as the talent will live on for many a generation.